contemporary graphic art in **poland**

graphic art in
poland

Richard Noyce

CRAFTSMAN HOUSE
G+B Arts International

Distributed in Australia by Craftsman House,
Tower A, 112 Talavera Road, North Ryde, Sydney NSW 2113
in association with G+B Arts International:
Australia, Canada, China, France, Germany,
India, Japan, Luxembourg, Malaysia,
The Netherlands, Russia, Singapore, Switzerland,
United Kingdom, United States of America

ISBN 90 5703 48 16

LOT Polish Airlines is proud to be involved in the production of *Contemporary Graphic Art in Poland*. Just as Polish graphics and printmaking are acclaimed across the globe as wonderful ambassadors for contemporary Polish life, so LOT strives to be such an ambassador for its country. LOT is a modern, sophisticated airline, catering to a world-wide market increasingly interested in all that Poland has to offer, not the least of which are the galleries of contemporary graphic art which can be found across the country.

Poland is a country which has never been afraid of interpreting itself to the public through various forms of media. Many of the works in *Contemporary Graphic Art in Poland* highlight the strength of this most modern of artforms, which so vividly portrays the intricate history and themes of Poland. As patrons of such works, all of us at LOT hope you enjoy the book as much as we have.

Design   Caroline de Fries
Layout   Craig Peterson
Printer   Kyodo Printing Co., Singapore

frontispiece: Jan Dobrkowski, *Uniwersum XV* (detail), 1992.
Watercolour on paper, 48 x 63 cm. Collection of the artist

Contents

Acknowledgments

This book represents the continuation of the work I began in 1993 on writing *Contemporary Painting in Poland*. To have become in the process ever more deeply involved in the Polish art scene has been a stimulating and fulfilling experience, convincing me yet further of the vitality and originality of Polish contemporary art. In researching and writing this second book I have received much encouragement from many people in Poland, England and Australia, to all of whom I am indebted for their wholehearted support.

In particular I wish to thank Jan Motyka and his colleagues at the Library of the Polish Academy of Sciences in Krakow — the Director of the Library, Dr Karolina Grodziska; and the Curator of the Print Room, Krzysztof Kruzel. Jan Motyka's assistance in collecting portfolios of artists' work greatly helped me during my visits to Krakow, as has the assistance he has given me during the writing of this book. I am also grateful to Jan Fejkiel of the Galeria Jan Fejkiel and Janina Gorka-Czarnecka of the Galeria Artemis, both in Krakow, for the help they gave me in so many ways; likewise Nina Rozwadowska of the Galeria Grafiki i Plakatu and Miroslawa Arens of the Galeria Zapiecek in Warsaw. The friendship over many years of Pawel Chawinski and Bozena Burzym-Chawinska of Krakow and the extensive assistance they gave me during the research for this book are warmly acknowledged. I wish to thank the management of the Jan III Sobieski Hotel in Warsaw for their hospitality and Dr Michal Praszalowicz for his assistance in enabling me to stay at the Guest House of the Jagiellonian University in Krakow. The continuing support for my work from Dr Hanna Mausch of the Polish Cultural Institute in London is valued as is the generous help given to me by Andrzej Rode, the United Kingdom and Ireland General Manager of LOT Polish Airlines in London, in arranging my journeys to Poland. Nevill Drury and his colleagues at Craftsman House in Sydney have continued to give invaluable and professional help during the production of this book, and I thank them. The artists featured in this book gave willingly of their time in the provision of information and in warm hospitality in their studios, giving me not only encouragement but also a wealth of knowledge of the intricacies of the Polish art world.

Finally I wish to thank my wife Fiona and my son Joseph for their continuing tolerance and good-humoured support over the past four years, during which Poland and Polish art have been a major part not only of my life, but theirs also.

Richard Noyce

Graphic art – an introduction

The primacy of painting and sculpture in the visual arts has, towards the end of this century, been eroded by a new questioning of values and those forms of art such as drawing and the production of sketchbooks, for some centuries considered to be little more than a preliminary stage in the production of major paintings, have come to the fore once more, but in terms very different from those prevalent from the Renaissance onwards. Durer, Michelangelo and da Vinci used drawing in a range of media to explore the ways in which their inner vision could become manifest, not only as a means of study for a later work in paint but as an end in themselves. The watercolours and drawings of Durer, for example, derived from his obsessive search for an explanation of how he could portray the wonders he saw around him, remain as evidence of the skill with which he impressed greatly those early 16th-century Italian artists who saw him working on his visit to Venice. These exquisite and often small works, and of course the magnificent drawings of Leonardo da Vinci, remain as a testament not only to the genius of these artists in their use of materials but also to their continual quest for the means for expressing their interpretation of the world in which they lived.

In the following centuries, as the patronage of artists shifted away from that of the Church to that of the emerging mercantile princes, drawing was still used by artists in the development of their work, but was seldom considered by the new patrons as an art form as valid as that of painting; the perceived 'value' was less. Such a perception remains embedded still in the taste of some present-day collectors, as evidenced by the prices reached at auction by drawings, which are usually much less than those commanded by paintings by the same artist. This is curious, because the immediacy and directness of the drawings of 18th- and 19th-century artists often demonstrates stronger evidence of their acute powers of perception than the paintings that resulted from such work.

In the field of printmaking, artists such as Rembrandt and Piranesi developed a high level of skill in the making of editions of etchings, but it was not until the 18th century that such prints achieved widespread popular success, and not just among wealthy connoisseurs; the work of satirists such as Hogarth and Gilray in England can be cited in this respect. With the development of new technology and artificial dyes in the 19th century, a consequence of the emergent industrialised urban society, the forms of expression available to young artists became more varied and with this change came new opportunities for gaining income. In this new world the work of artists such as Toulouse-Lautrec took a revolutionary direction and the modern poster was born with its bold forms, bright colours and the integration of lettering. The work of young artists began to gain a relevance beyond that of the confines of the Salon and the enclosed society of the connoisseurs — it became irrevocably part of the visual framework of the modern world. The scene was set for the art of the 20th century, with its succession of movements and styles, each responding in turn to the cataclysmic changes brought about by political upheavals and wars, leading to the confusion of the years following the Second World War, and on into the 1960s and 1970s when the visual arts entered what many critics believed to be a state of crisis. At one time it seemed that the popularising of art, and of Pop Art in particular, was about to bring to an end the steady evolution of artistic styles and replace it with art as a cheap and expendable decorative commodity.

In response to this sense of crisis, amounting in the view of some artists to the engendering of a state of near-total deracination with their consequent refusal to accept the need to refer, even in a peripheral sense, to the work of artists in previous centuries, new forms of expression emerged that were devoid of any use of the traditional media such as mere paint or pencil. Happenings, those quasi-theatrical events that took Dadaism to its final and logical conclusion of everything happening all at once, seemed in the late 1960s to threaten the viability of traditional art forms. Writing to me in December 1967 Allan Kaprow, one of the main American progenitors of happenings, stated: 'I'd say physical needs must be satisfied before *anyone* wants to think about art; old art forms were responses to real environments, as our new forms are to this environment; thus the older ones serve only our nostalgic needs; planned obsolescence in production is a model for our arts; the *idea* of permanence embodied in a perishable form is the only viable irony possible today'. Thirty years later the irony has been reversed and happenings as an art form have been consigned to history, themselves serving the nostalgic needs of those who experienced them.

In the following three decades new forms of art have emerged, each offering new means of expression to artists. Minimalism, which reduced the appearance of the end product to its bare bones, Conceptual Art, in which even the object disappeared into a seemingly endless succession of ideas and texts impenetrable to all but a self-appointed coterie of intellectuals and, finally, Installations, which often served to obfuscate rather than enlighten the observer, became the mega-dollar currency on which the gallery worlds of Western Europe and the United States thrived briefly. However, the distance between the creators of such art and their patrons on the one hand and the general art-loving public on the other widened to a gulf into which much of this art eventually sank. The critics' announcement of the crisis in art was perhaps premature, but it did serve to engender such art which, even from the perspective of relatively few years in time, can now be seen to have been vacuous and self-defeating. Postmodernism, a catch-all description without adequate definition, was heralded as the solution to the confusion bringing such forms of expression as seen in the work of Damien Hirst and Jeff Koons which persist still, but which may not retain their limited relevance to the gallery-going public or their attraction to the new collectors for much longer. To the general public, thanks to such artists' flair for self-publicity, such work remains little more than a very expensive joke. Perhaps this will come to be seen by future art historians as one of the intended outcomes of such art, in which the concepts of long-term durability of the art work and the possibility of its survival into the future are no longer relevant — a form of art equivalent to fast food and the ephemeral world of high fashion. For all the glamour that the new art attached to itself and for all the excessive sums of money that artists and their galleries earned through their endeavours, its role and importance in the long history of the visual arts may in due time be seen to be very small indeed.

Despite the confusion and apathy that the production of the new art has brought there has remained a persistent and undeniable undercurrent of visual art produced in more or less traditional ways, and it can be argued that it is through this production, and not that of the exponents of Minimalism and Conceptual Art, as well as that of their lesser followers, that the art of the 21st century will develop. The possibilities of new media derived from the continuing developments of technology, computer technology in particular, will of course influence the work of artists, and there are indications that this is beginning to achieve a more mature result than the early experiments in the medium might have suggested was possible. The traditional media of painting and drawing, and the related media of printmaking, have regained their importance and through this can be seen a return to more traditional forms, albeit a return coloured by a changing perception of the moral and philosophical imperatives of the visual arts as we approach the next millennium.

In Poland, as in other countries in Eastern Europe which were for almost half a century isolated behind the Iron Curtain, it has become apparent that the corrosive effects of the commercialisation and cynicism that affected the visual arts in the Western world have had a much less far-reaching effect. Artists working in such countries, although they understandably felt a sense of frustration through being cut off from what was happening elsewhere, had the opportunity to develop their work from more traditional roots and with a personally relevant sense of the history of their country and its culture. The result can be seen to have a different vitality, but one which is well suited to the changing world into which they now, thankfully, have the chance to emerge. The work they have produced over the past fifty years can be seen to belong to a long continuum of artistic production, essentially part of, and not divorced from, the mainstream of world art history.

This book, written as a partner to my first book, *Contemporary Painting in Poland*, seeks to explore further the ways in which Polish artists have developed their approaches to the visual arts and the high quality of the work that has resulted. As with the previous publication this book does not seek to be the final critical definition of an aspect of Polish art in the recent past, for which a longer historical perspective will be required, but rather a record, which it is hoped will be timely, of a remarkable level of achievement in the first half of the 1990s; a record which has a well-established history of antecedents and which deserves to be more widely appreciated in world terms.

The Polishness of Polish contemporary art

As with the art of any country, the art of Poland cannot be seen in isolation from history or social development. In any country there are always artists who follow the officially sanctioned lines, whether they be those of state *diktat* or the norms of what is considered acceptable by the establishment. Likewise, there are always artists who go against the official view, whose work owes its nature to deeply held beliefs in the value of art as art (rather than as a cultural prop to the state or establishment) and which is in essence revolutionary. Poland, more than most European countries, has suffered a century of upheaval in which even the borders of the country have shifted more than once. Due largely to the geographical position of their country Poles have had to learn to adapt and change to altered circumstances, not once but many times. At the same time, through the lessons of the past, Poles have come to value deeply their cultural identity — based on an awareness of history and a pride in the country's achievements. The paintings of Matejko in the 19th century, of Malczewski at the turn of the century, as well as the work of the avant-garde in the 1920s and 1930s, have all provided a basis from which much of 20th-century Polish art has sprung. Add to this historical pride the rich diversity of cultural influences in the country — Germanic influences from the west, Slavic influences from the east, Bohemian influences from the south and Baltic influences from the north, all tempered with a pervasive awareness of Catholicism (if not its active pursuit) — and there is a rich ferment which predisposes the development of highly individual art.

It cannot be denied that the influence of contemporary art in other countries has had some effect on the art that is being developed in Poland, although this has not, through the relative unavailability of information during the Communist era, been a major influence until fairly recently: with the fall of Communism and the consequent rapid social changes in the country it may now become a factor of growing importance. The comparative scarcity of materials and information on world art developments during the 1970s and 1980s was often a cause for regret among young Polish artists, and yet I believe that, far from deadening their progress, this lack became an incentive to make the best art possible from limited resources. The situation is changing and will continue to do so, but it is to be hoped that the ability of Poles to draw on their own resources, rather than to allow themselves to become absorbed into some sort of pan-European identity, will allow the development of art that remains essentially Polish.

It is more difficult to define what this 'Polishness' is. It certainly owes much to aspects of the Polish character as evidenced in daily life, such as an open generosity of spirit, a warm hospitality to guests, a remarkable sense of humour that tends to manifest itself in an ironic self-deprecation, and an obstinate refusal to conform totally to demands imposed from outside. There is also the continuation of a very long intellectual tradition in which questions regarding the philosophy of art are of perennial concern. Few Western European countries, particularly those who in the 20th century have been comparatively untroubled by war and social upheaval, have the same regard for art criticism. Few English people would, for example, give their profession as 'critic of art', as many do in Poland.

In looking at Polish art over the past quarter century from the point of view of an outsider I have been increasingly fascinated by its central strength and vitality. Now that a time of growing freedom has at last come to Poland I hope that the strengths that have nurtured its art in the past will continue to nurture its future. A blurring of these strengths through the imitation of international fashion shifts would be much to be regretted, but it seems at present that this is not very likely to happen. Obstinacy has its merits …

Diversity and substance

It would be foolish to attempt to divide the art of any nation into neat categories. In so doing the nuances of difference would be lost and with them much of the vital character of that art. While it may be simple from a basic perspective to state that the art of one artist is 'figurative' and that of another is 'abstract', the truth is usually more subtle. Indeed, during a long career, an artist may go through a series of changes in approach and in so doing produce work that seems close to one style one year and to another the next. Therefore, defining an artist as belonging exclusively to one category or another is an exercise in limited perception. This assertion is true for any art form but in the case of graphic art is particularly so. The directness of the graphic arts, based as they are on the drawn line, renders them less simply definable as being of one style or another, for every image is essentially an abstraction from the experience of the artist, whether in perceived reality or the imagination, noted down simply or created through a process of interior reflection and the techniques of the print studio.

The diversity of work selected for this book is intentionally wide, seeking to offer for consideration work produced in the past five years or so by Polish artists in the graphic arts. This diversity should be seen as representative of some of the ways in which they approach the making of art. Many of the artists are also active in other forms of art such as painting and may adopt an approach that is very different in those forms. This is not to say that the output of such artists lacks coherence, rather that they choose various means at different times and for many individual reasons. This fact is one of the main reasons for the vitality of contemporary art and in Poland is underpinned by a number of factors that are peculiarly Polish. Among these are the extremes of social and political change through which the artists have lived and the process of evolution through which their country is presently going, but perhaps the most important is the underlying presence of Catholicism. This is not to say that there is a distinctly 'religious' aspect to Polish art: in a few cases this may be so, but such an overt aspect does not appear among the artists in this book. Notwithstanding this there is a strong element that is common in the work of many of the artists that may be seen as a parallel influence.

Many artists in their writings, and critics likewise, refer to the 'sacrum' in art, as opposed to the 'profanum'. These terms do not simply mean the sacred and the profane as referred to in religious faith, but rather to something with a deeper philosophical sense that is just as present in art but which is not specifically religious in content, meaning or intention. The recurrence of the words 'sacrum', and to a lesser extent 'profanum', is indicative of an awareness in the artists not only of the legacy of Catholicism which has been instrumental in enabling much of the change in the country in recent years (a legacy that is accorded its due place), but also an awareness of a deeper and richer heritage from beyond the confines of a single form of religious faith. It is, in short, an awareness of the essential task of the artist — that of responding to the essence of the creative act, of producing work that seeks to illuminate a personal vision of the realm of the perceived and the imagined through the making of art.

The work presented in this book exhibits a great diversity of approaches, a superficial analysis of which may enable them to be divided into 'figurative', 'abstract' and so on: to do so would be to ignore the deeper and more subtle threads that unite them. Among these must of course be the unity that defines them as 'Polish' but, importantly, the work should be seen as having a substance that has much to do with the quest for a personal response to the 'sacrum'. While some of the artists are more closely aware of international trends than others, all show in their work a common sense of the seriousness of the creative act, whatever the first impression of their work may be. Through a wide range of styles and approaches these artists demonstrate fully the sublime essence of what it is to make art and to express this by means which may at first be seen as deeply serious on the one hand or exuberant in their lightness on the other. Whatever the first impression may be there is no doubt that all the artists are aware of the power of the 'sacrum' and their need to give this power expression. This may appear to some as being of no great general value (and art criticism, rooted as it is in a complex of theories, may even discount it as being too much of a broad generalisation) but it can also be seen as being the root from which all true art must spring. As a Zen Master said: 'Laugh, there is nothing serious in Life: be serious, there is nothing humorous in Life' — a paradoxical truth that may also be applied to the work of these Polish artists, demonstrating levity and gravity in full and equal measure.

Contemporary Polish graphic art – a general introduction

The artists using graphic art as a major medium in their work who are featured in this book provide a representative selection of all such artists working in Poland today. Some have already established reputations, others are less well known, but taken together they offer an overview of the vitality of Polish graphic art. That there are omissions has been inevitable — the number of good artists is considerable but all could not be included. Omission is by no means an indication of a lack of worth; indeed, the quality of the work of such artists is equal to those who have been included. This should be seen as indicative of one of the strengths of Polish art and will, it is hoped, prompt others to explore the diversity of this work for themselves.

As with other forms of visual art in Poland, there is a strong tradition of established artists working in the Academies of Fine Art and other further educational establishments. Thus it is that something akin to the 'master–apprentice' system has evolved in which tradition and innovation are equally encouraged. It is usual for Polish artists' curricula vitae to include the names of those professors under whom they have studied. This makes it possible to trace back through a considerable period of time the influences which each generation has had on the others. It might be thought that this would engender a derivative situation in which only a slow evolution has been possible — far from this it has proved to be a fertile field in which healthy innovation has been encouraged as an active part of the educational process.

At the same time other influences have come to bear on the development of graphic art in the recent past. As with all forms of artistic endeavour, the changing social and political situation in the country during the past fifteen years has had a profound effect on the art that has been produced. There are instances, referred to in the texts on individual artists, of powerful socio-political comments being made, some overtly and others in a more subtle but nonetheless potent fashion. The effect of work by former generations of artists on the emerging young generation cannot be discounted. While some of these artists are well known, there are others for whom recognition has been limited. As in any country, there are artists who have seldom had exposure on the international scene and who may have achieved little public success, for one reason or another, even in their own country. Nonetheless, such artists have often had a strong influence on others with whom they have come into contact. In addition, the growing impact of artists working in other countries must be taken into account now that far greater access to information on their work is widely available. These threads of influence can be seen to have had much to do with the strong and energetic visual arts scene in Poland today.

fine art printmaking in poland

Printmaking as a fine art form has long been a mainstay of the Polish art scene. For many artists who have pursued their art through the medium of painting, or that of drawing as a discrete art form or as an adjunct to painting, the making of editioned prints has been a parallel discipline which has offered them an alternative means for the expression of their art. For others printmaking itself has been the main form, giving these artists a preoccupation with the creation of editioned works, sometimes, but not always, accompanied by the making of finished drawings. The sheer variety of styles of printmaking is at first bewildering and the number of artists who are actively engaged in this medium is astonishing. For example, Krakow alone has a large number of artists: the main Artists' Union has some 1500 members with an interest in all forms of art. Even if only 10 per cent (and this is doubtless a considerable underestimate) of these members are actively engaged at any time in making and showing their art, many being practising printmakers, this is a remarkable number for a medium-sized city (albeit one that has long been the visual arts 'capital' of Poland). A similar situation is repeated in all the major cities of Poland, with notable centres being the national capital of Warsaw, in which a very varied and active arts scene has developed since the Second World War; the grim and polluted industrial Katowice area, which nonetheless has an impressive visual arts record; a small but important centre in the southern mountain town of Zakopane, where traditional folk art and contemporary practice have blended together to give a unique style; and the former textile city of Lodz. This long-established industrial city in the heart of Poland also boasts the world-famous Lodz School of Film Forms whose graduates include many famous film makers such as Wajda, Polanski and Kieslowski, as well as being the centre in which the seminally important artist and theoretician Wladyslaw Strzeminski did much of his work. The influences that come from this diverse cultural context cannot be discounted. In other Polish cities such as Wroclaw, Gdansk and Lublin, as well as in comparatively remote towns such as Przemysl (each having their own unique cultural history and aided by the network of galleries established by the state under the former centralised system of government), there are equally distinct and lively visual arts scenes which nurture much fine work in printmaking as well as in other forms of the visual arts.

It is a characteristic of the Polish arts scene that different centres have tended to develop individual identities and, with this, a sense of rivalry. Notable in this respect is the situation of Warsaw and Krakow, between which until comparatively recently there was little interchange of exhibitions and critical dialogue. The reasons for this may be traced to the historical partition of the country in the 19th century, as well as to the social and political disruptions of the past fifty years. However, there are signs that, at last, there is the beginning of a softening of the critical stance and a recognition of the considerable contribution that each has made to the national scene. Paradoxically, at the same time as rivalries tended to keep artists in different areas apart, there has been a growing Polish national presence on the international arts scene through the participation of numerous artists in both large and small print festivals and in group and individual exhibitions, with many of these artists gaining success in winning major awards and a growing international recognition of their achievements. Poland itself is building a fine reputation for the initiation and development of exhibitions of printmaking, particularly with the success of the International Print Triennale of Krakow (showing in 1997 and again in 2000) and its growing number of associated exhibitions within Poland and elsewhere. This exhibition has grown in importance and now has a major influence, creating a regular focus for Polish artists as well as those from many other parts of the world. This curious combination of introspection coupled with a strong presence on the international scene has led to a strength and vitality in Polish printmaking that will allow its further development with growing confidence.

There is a long tradition in Poland of printmaking in conventional media. In this respect there has been much fine work in intaglio techniques, both etching and engraving, with an emphasis on drawing as the basis for development. Equally there has been much fine work in the creation of linocuts,

and a distinctively Polish style in this difficult medium has emerged. To a lesser, but nonetheless important, extent techniques such as wood engraving and cutting and silkscreen printing have been developed. In recent years there has been much experimenting with all these forms, and in particular with their combination, both in traditional manner and in conjunction with their newer counterparts. As the availability of computers has increased, the variety of forms of electronic imaging technique is being explored within printmaking to good effect, and this development is likely to continue, introducing an important new element into the range of available forms. The strong academic tradition in the visual arts, with its powerful sense of the value of the past, and a concurrent record of continuing innovation have combined to create a context in which not only has much fine work been achieved already but in which Polish artists are well placed to develop their work into the next century with growing assurance and international relevance.

drawing in poland

Drawing as a pure art form occupies a position in Polish art that is secure and of continuing importance. The inclusion of regular studio sessions of drawing in the academies has long provided a backbone to courses of all types, as part of the training in painting, sculpture, design and printmaking. Drawing is an ancient, even primitive, skill in which there is an immediate attraction in the act of drawing that reveals more intimately the external result of an internal process than processes such as painting or printmaking, which require more skill in the manipulation of technique and which often require a longer process of change and development to bring them to a conclusion. Drawing can be seen as an essentially simple act — the making of direct marks with basic means — and at the same time can achieve a high level of artistic and intellectual sophistication. That it remains central to all academic training is an important element in the continuing Polish tradition. By contrast, in some other parts of the world in the recent past drawing has not been accorded so important a place in the development of creative ability, or has even been ignored in colleges of art. The result of this can be seen in paintings and other art forms that frequently have a lack of the depth and potency that comes with a training in drawing from the cast, or from the figure, which enables the acquisition of a skill in observation and recording of form that cannot be acquired so easily or so directly in any other way. In addition, drawing is a skill that can be practised without the need for specialised studios or equipment and is not so dependent on the scale of the finished work for its impact. Small drawings can be produced simply and at any time or in any place and can have as much power as large paintings or technically complex prints.

The range of drawing produced by Polish artists is very wide, covering everything from small satirical drawings to over-life-sized figurative portraits, and in a range of materials that includes pencil, graphite, charcoal and ink, often in combination. Sometimes watercolour is used, although not as frequently as in other parts of Europe that have a longer tradition in this particular medium. The resultant work is often figurative, whether it is due to the return to figuration that characterises much painting in Poland or the inherent adaptability of drawing to this form of expression. It is significant that many artists in Poland make use of sketch-books or workbooks using primarily drawing as an ongoing means of recording otherwise potentially fugitive impressions and ideas. Access to these books can be a very illuminating experience which demonstrates well the manner in which final forms have been reached and it is a matter of some regret that they are seldom seen as part of contemporary exhibitions.

Drawing is a gentle form of art that makes less demand on the viewer than painting or printmaking. It often results in small forms that are perceived by some as being merely illustrations. Many galleries, whether commercial or public, have in the past relegated artists' drawings to the position of footnotes to their paintings and this has in turn affected the perception of collectors. All of which are causes for regret as drawing can, and in the case of Polish art, frequently does, achieve just as much as the more highly regarded forms. The work shown by Polish artists in this book serves to prove this fact.

poster art in poland

During the 1970s and 1980s posters achieved one of the internationally recognised high points of Polish art. The quantity and quality of the output was considerable and through this medium a great deal of social and political criticism was possible. There is a paradox in the making of posters, evidenced particularly in Poland, in that the poster is essentially ephemeral, serving to publicise an event or a statement related to a particular situation. The poster appears, serves its purpose and is then replaced by others with a more immediate importance. However, the sheer vitality and originality of Polish posters from these decades has rendered them eminently collectable and many have survived as art objects in their own right. In addition, while the production of good quality illustrated art books and exhibition

catalogues was limited, the high standard of printing of such posters gave them a quality which has enabled many examples to survive well past the reach of their original purpose.

The rapidly changing social and political situation in Poland in the past twenty years mobilised some of the finest work by artists, and graphic artists in particular found a powerful source of ideas and imagery. The state-run promotion of film and theatre, for example, gave a great deal of work to poster artists who used the commissions they received not only to produce some memorable posters for the productions themselves but also to introduce elements that were inherently critical of the contemporary situation. At the height of this phase as many as three hundred commissions a year for film alone were given to artists. Productions of plays such as *King Lear* and *Macbeth* by Shakespeare gave the opportunity to comment on events in present-day Poland, while the interpretation of American films such as *Platoon* and *Someone to Watch Over Me* were startlingly original and contrasted greatly with the images used on posters for these films in Western Europe and the United States. The most powerful images, however, came from posters publicising indigenous Polish film and theatre productions, and for posters intended to publicise ecological and social concerns, where the full force of the artists' use of biting satire could be employed to memorable effect.

The potency of such work relies greatly on a form of surrealism and, in many cases, it dispenses with the elegant typography that typifies poster art in the West in favour of hand-drawn lettering. These elements, combined with a powerful use of colour, produced images that retain an undeniable power long after the original purpose for which they were made. It is certain that one of the major forces in publicising the rise of Solidarity in the early 1980s came from the hand-painted logo of the name *Solidarnosc* which incorporated the Polish flag in a way that had never been used before. This style of lettering was later used to good effect in a number of posters, linking the events which they publicised with the political aims of Solidarity. Another important element in the poster art from this period comes from the nature of Polish humour, where self-mockery and irony are typical. Just as it is said that the best Jewish jokes are told by Jewish people and Irish jokes by the Irish, so the best jokes by Poles themselves transcend the humour of Polish jokes told by others: self-deprecation is indeed a powerful method of putting a serious point across.

The fall of Communism seems to have had the effect of slowing down the output of such original and powerful posters. The opening out to Western influences has brought with it the transformation of advertising and the growth of agencies, whether Polish or branches of American and British firms, has been rapid. There is now often little to distinguish advertising in Poland from that in Britain and the United States, the products are the same, whether consumer goods or entertainment, and the images and production values in posters and press advertisements are frequently identical. Consumerism on the Western model has gained a secure foothold, rendering the previous 'them and us' situation invalid. In many ways this can be seen as being inevitable as the country emerges from a darker past to regain its full place on a European stage, but it is nonetheless a matter of some regret that the originality of Polish poster art appears to have fallen victim to the international norm. The work of excellent artists that once produced powerfully critical posters is now more frequently seen in the pages of Polish editions of international consumer and leisure magazines.

the future

This book has been written and published towards the end of a century which has seen Poland undergoing a major evolution, from a state subjugated to imperialism to an independent nation, then through a cataclysmic war and a long period of totalitarian absorption into the Communist block before its emergence as an independent nation once more, this time with a rapidly developing free-market economy. The art produced during the 20th century will be seen to have responded to these changes and the social tragedies and upheavals that accompanied them. The perception of Polish art in the West has been limited by the scarcity of information on what has been produced and, indeed, even within the country itself, little of the considerable achievement has been realised fully. Poland's emergence coincides with a less than easy evolution in international economics and society and many of the problems that Poland faces are replicated in other countries.

The art that is produced in any country cannot be seen in isolation from the situation in which it has developed and is subject to a complex process of understanding that requires a distance in time for a full and complete analysis. This book does not set out to do more than offer for consideration an eclectic selection of work produced in the past few years by Polish artists of all contemporary generations for whom printmaking, drawing and posters have a major role in their work. It is of course work that has developed from a much longer historical continuum and sound traditions. What will develop in the future is largely dependent on the manner in which Poland's transition is successful, but also in the degree

to which a wider international appreciation of Polish art is obtained. Regardless of these factors it seems very likely that the achievements that are shown in this book, as well as those of the many artists producing work of similar quality, will continue and will develop. There is an inherent strength in Polish art which shows no sign of diminution and this will ensure that further development will be possible. The new sense of optimism that has emerged in Poland in recent years, even coloured as it is by uncertainties and a degree of healthy scepticism, will be reflected in the art that is produced in the future. It seems very likely that the potential for Polish art will merit optimism.

Bogdan **Achimescu**

Romanian by birth, Bogdan Achimescu was born in Timisoara in 1965 where he studied at the Ion Vidu High School of Arts, later completing his studies at the Academy of Fine Arts in Cluj. In 1990 he moved to Krakow and completed a year of studies at the Jagiellonian University before studying at the Academy of Fine Arts for three years, graduating from the printmaking studio of the influential Professor Stanislaw Wejman in 1993. He taught at the Academy from 1993–94 and at the Skowhegan School of Painting and Sculpture in the United States during 1995. He now divides his time between Timisoara and Krakow, cities that have both known in their own ways the effects of human cruelty. His personal background and training give him an unusual place in the art world of Poland, as does his espousal of an eclectic range of media which includes drawing, installation and computer-generated art as well as printmaking.

In common with a number of other young Polish contemporaries, Achimescu chooses to push the limits of his techniques to the full, and while his printmaking is centred on the very traditional technique of etching, his approach has the effect of limiting the possibilities of large editions, frequently resulting in a single print. Although he may start in a traditional way, the resulting image is not a straightforward etching as it incorporates broad areas of paint. Not for him the purity of the etched line and carefully controlled tonal areas: his approach is far more that of a rebel who seeks through unconventional means the possibilities of the creation of a powerful image, a process that is perhaps closer to that of painting. As such he provides through his work a new direction for Polish printmaking which complements the manner in which he approaches his use of other media, and also the way in which a significant number of other Polish artists of the same generation have adopted an iconoclastic attitude towards the achievements of the past. There are many precedents for this attitude in the history of 20th century Polish art, some of which have since become recognised as mainstays of the tradition of the avant-garde in that country.

Achimescu's work in printmaking is first and foremost figurative, based on the human figure, frequently nude. In choosing this most basic and ancient of forms he allies himself with the human condition, an alignment that, considering his background, is all the more poignant. He portrays his figures standing, sitting or crouched, in stances that suggest their vulnerability and also their potential. Their faces look outwards, towards and past the viewer; their bodily positions, although fixed, demonstrate their ability to move onwards. In this they are essentially optimistic, accepting their present circumstances yet awaiting the changes that will lead them forward. In some of his works portraying the human head Achimescu adopts an alternative position, that of showing the head, detached from any visible body. With eyes shut these heads hold within them the silence and reflective thought of the contemplative; they become mysterious, revealing nothing of their thoughts. As an extension of the artist's thinking they also reveal an alternative view to that of his figures, a view that is entirely complementary.

In some of his works dating from the early 1990s Achimescu combines heads and figures. *Without Title*, 1992, shows two heads, their eyes closed, or blank like the eyes of archaic Greek statues, African masks or Modigliani drawings, with five figures shown crouching, their hands to their faces — the eighth part of this work is blank, leading the viewer to construct a meaning for the combination of etched forms. Basic emotions are shown or implied, there are tensions and possibilities for some sort of resolution, but the total effect is one of bleakness, as if speaking of an insoluble problem. This large (70 cm x 100 cm) print was awarded the Grand Prix at the 1993 Premio Internazionale per l'Incisione at Biella in Italy, significant perhaps at a time of change from the dire conditions of former years in his native country.

Achimescu's art is rebellious and challenges many of the conventions of his adopted city. Yet it provides ample evidence of the possibilities for change, and the tolerance of them, that have so long nurtured the best in Polish art. While young, he provides sufficient evidence to suggest that his future work in a country whose horizons are expanding holds much promise for an artist whose own horizons are not limited by convention.

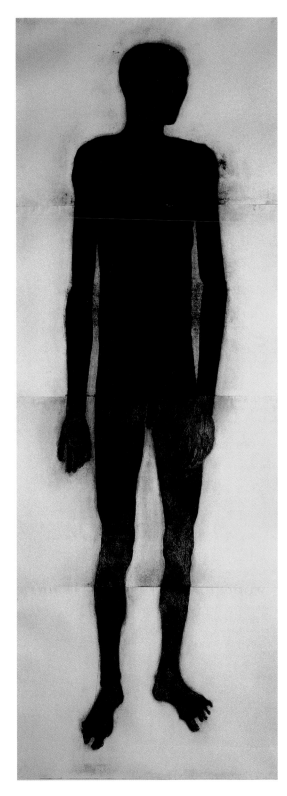

Bogdan Achimescu **Wczesnak (Born Early)**
1993, Monotype etching, 250 x 92 cm.
Private collection, Krakow. Photograph: Marek Gardulski

Bogdan Achimescu **TDB sur C**
1996, Etching, 56 x 60 cm. Collection: Print Room of the Polish Academy of Sciences, Krakow. Photograph: Pawel Chawinski

Bogdan Achimescu **Negr…**
1994, Monotype etching, 65 x 49 cm. Photograph: courtesy of the Jan Fejkiel Gallery, Krakow

Grzegorz **Banaszkiewicz**

Grzegorz Banaszkiewicz was born in Czestochowa in 1951 and graduated from the studio of Professor Mieczyslaw Wejman at the Krakow Academy of Fine Arts in 1976, where he studied for five years from 1971. He is a lecturer in the Faculty of Art Education at the Pedagogic High School in Czestochowa and is active in printmaking, drawing, graphic design and photography. He lives in Krakow and has exhibited widely in Poland and many other countries.

His work in the past fifteen years has been very personal in its approach and is exclusively based on figuration. Family portraits, railway engines, portraits of local characters, fragments of the built environment, self-portraits and remnants of Krakow's past all recur throughout his work. He is a highly skilled draughtsman whose drawings achieve a near photographic intensity, showing a mastery of the manipulation of tone and infinite care in execution. While clearly derived from photographs, they are not lacking in warmth: indeed, the painstaking rendition of the fugitive shifts of light and shade, which can be frozen or lost in photographs, imbues his drawings with a subtle degree of imprecision that renders them all the more memorable. He has harnessed, to a high degree, the camera's ability to select and present a moment in time, but he transfers this through the hours of work required to make a drawing into a powerfully evocative crystallisation of not just that moment itself but also the existence of his selected subjects in the time before the photograph was taken.

This potent awareness of the nature of time and the place of his subjects within it is even more apparent in his printmaking, in which he uses a range of delicately controlled processes (lithography, photo-lithography and aquatint among them) to recreate the deep essence of his initial material. For example, in *Machine du Temps*, a lithograph of 1993, he presents a sequence of family portraits reaching back into history and emerging from a textured surface which in turn comes from the smokestacks of a curiously doubled image of an old railway engine. The effect is haunting, capturing a succession of moments in time combined with the surreal image of a train pulling in both directions — the passing of time is shown with great potency. In *Murs d'Anvers*, another lithograph from the same year (not illustrated here), the image is superficially more straightforward: a wall with the crackled stucco of age provides the ground within which a disused letterbox flap can be seen and over which is superimposed the face of a woman that looks out beyond the viewer with a cool and intense expression. The connections that can be made are deeper, less apparent, but nonetheless achieve something akin to the abstract power of poetry.

13 Exercises de Litho à Anvers, 1993, utilises a similar technique but this time in a more complex manner. The textures of the wall are more varied and in this lithograph it is the artist's face that gazes out, engaging the viewer's attention. To the right of this double image is a regular grid of twelve demonstrations of the variations of effect that are possible in lithography through the use of different techniques. The artist places himself, and his ability in the use of those techniques, clearly within the history of a specific place that is implied through the overlaying of textures in the wall that rises from the weeds at its base. Through this combination of elements one can discern the artist stating his identity within the history of a time and place. This can be seen also in *Mur de Lamentation*, 1990, a photo-etching of the Wailing Wall in the Cemetery of the Remuh Synagogue in Krakow's Kazimierz district, the old Jewish quarter and former ghetto which was almost completely destroyed during the Second World War. Banaszkiewicz presents the wall, which is built from ancient tombstones salvaged from the destruction, as a powerful monument to a tragic past that is still too hard to comprehend fully. By choosing a low viewpoint and by a skilful manipulation of technique, the wall is shown not with its surrounding buildings but against a clouded sky through which the light breaks. It is a statement that is direct and poetic, but which does not lapse into romanticism, paying due respect to the past and at the same time provoking many questions about both the present and the future. With such sureness of approach combined with consummate technical skill Banaszkiewicz is an artist fully engaged with the true matter of art.

Grzegorz Banaszkiewicz **Mur de Lamentation**
1990, Photo etching, 69 x 44 cm. Collection of the artist

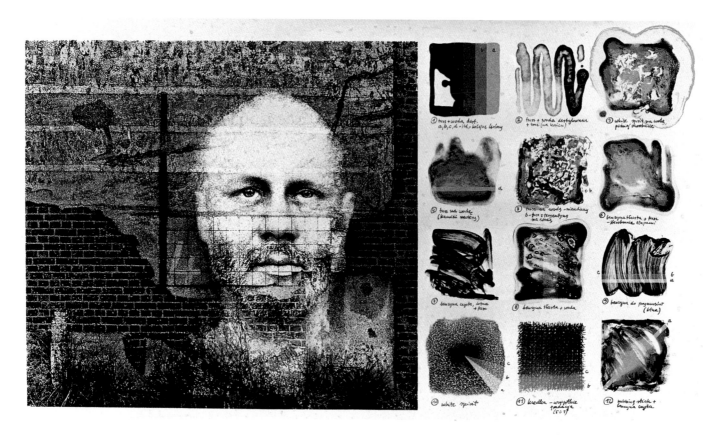

Grzegorz Banaszkiewicz **13 Exercises de Litho à Anvers**

1993, Lithograph, 40 x 70 cm. Grand Prix: Print of the month competition, Krakow 1993. Collection of the artist

Grzegorz Banaszkiewicz **Machine du Temps**
1993, Lithograph 65.5 x 56.5 cm. Collection of the artist

Andrzej **Bebenek**

Born in Chrzanow in 1950, Andrzej Bebenek studied at the Academy of Fine Arts in Krakow, graduating from the gravure studio of Professor Mieczyslaw Wejman, whose influence as an artist and teacher has been crucial to the development of printmaking in that city. From 1977–80 Bebenek was a lecturer in Professor Andrzej Pietsch's class at the Academy and since then has been an Associate Professor and Director of the Arts Department at the Institute of Arts Education in the Higher Pedagogical College in Krakow. His activity as an artist encompasses painting and sculpture as well as printmaking.

Central to Bebenek's art is his preoccupation with the form of the rhombus, which occurs as the main element in his work in all media. While such elemental forms as the circle, square and triangle recur throughout the natural and built environments, the rhombus, for all its geometric purity, is more of an artificial construct, with a different essential dynamism, hinting at an alternative concept of space. In an 'action' that took place early one morning in May 1992 the artist superimposed a large rhombus made from wide strips of white paper on the squared pattern of the paving in the Rynek Glowny, Krakow's huge Market Square. He placed his form on the diagonal between the ancient Church of St Adalbert and the medieval Sukiennice Market Hall, with one apex pointing towards the monumental statue of Poland's most celebrated national poet, Adam Mickiewicz. Each apex was anchored with a white rectangular block bearing a black rhombus. The photographs taken from the top of the towers of the Mariacki Church show Bebenek's form introducing a new geometry and a silent presence into one of Europe's most impressive and historically important urban spaces.

The sense of intervention characterises much of this artist's work. In the 1993 series of 'Objects' made from wood, metal and paint he uses the rigidity of three-dimensional geometric forms and the fluidity of the textures of colours that replicate those of the ageing of natural materials to set up a dialogue between these opposing yet complementary systems. Other free-standing sculptures create a similar dialogue with the spaces in which they are placed. In his paintings the use of fluid and joyful colours is interrupted by numbers of black rhombuses which suggest either superimposition of these forms or the presence of dark space through and beyond the surface of the painting: there is a certain sense of the duality between figure and ground, the creation of a layered illusion. Yet these methods of work are more than mere academic exercises in the manipulation of a deliberately limited repertoire of forms. They are indicative of a quest for the equilibrium that can be found between them and for the balance between the natural and created environment on the one hand and the imaginative power of the artist on the other.

In his printmaking Bebenek takes this investigation one stage further. The nature of the processes of etching and aquatint impose a different rigour on the artist, relying on the interaction of different materials and a degree of variation that requires greater control than that needed in the making of paintings and sculpture. By choosing to limit the size of his prints to 50 cm x 65 cm and the tones to pure black and greys, he narrows the possibilities considerably yet has at the same time found a sense of freedom that comes from this limitation. The black rhombus no longer has the hard edge of his work in other media but appears rather more transient. The tonal greys appear either to contain the black forms or to be encroaching on them. The tones contain lines and textures that come from the process itself or the artist's hand, allowing a consideration of the totality of the process that has created these dynamic images.

The work of Andrzej Bebenek may appear to be abstract, but it is also that of an artist whose sensibilities towards the essence of the natural and created worlds and that of the work of the imagination, as well as the inherent nature of his chosen materials, are fully controlled and will doubtless lead to further investigation.

Andrzej Bebenek **Sita I Noc (Strength and Force)**
1991, Etching and aquatint, 54 x 69.5 cm. Collection of the artist. Photograph: Pawel Chawinski

Andrzej Bebenek **Vanua Levu**
1990, Etching and aquatint, 50 x 65 cm. Collection of the artist

Andrzej Bebenek **Sluga Cierpliwosci**
1991, Etching and aquatint, 50 x 65 cm. Collection of the artist

Andrzej **Bednarczyk**

Andrzej Bednarczyk was born in 1960 in Lesna and is a graduate of the Krakow Academy of Fine Arts where he studied graphics and painting from 1981–86, completing his studies in the studio of Zbigniew Grzybowski. Since then he has met with considerable critical success and now couples his work as an assistant lecturer in the Academy's Department of Painting with his personal work in painting and graphics. He has also achieved success as a poet, and in 1995 published a unique book/art object, *The Temple of Stone*, which incorporates photography, die cut pages and a stone together with Polish/English text, bound in stone and string.

As a member of the younger generation of Polish artists Bednarczyk's work offers a view of the new Poland and has a freshness that results from his experience of growing to maturity under circumstances considerably different from those that faced artists of previous generations. Living and working in Krakow allows him the opportunity to participate in a cultural life that has a long and very distinguished history, one which encompasses music, philosophy and literature as much as the visual arts. From such a rich seed-bed he is producing work of great originality, combining a fascination with materials and a mysterious mysticism. His paintings, incorporating pure gold as well as base materials such as coal and grit, are justly celebrated, having both a monumental presence and allusions that link his work to a long continuum stretching back to Byzantine and Medieval art. He is meticulous in his working methods and his studio is a well-ordered set of spaces within which he works with a controlled enthusiasm for the possibilities of the colours and textures of paint, canvas and paper.

His drawings push forward the boundaries of the graphic form, turning them into something approaching sculpture rather than the simple making of lines on a flat surface and, yet, they remain essentially drawn. Heavy papers are compressed and combined, then torn or carved into fragmented forms, drawn on in pencil and ink, overlaid with colour or gold leaf, punched with holes, printed with graphic or photographic images of tools, scraps of material and fish and presented, some framed in the void between two sheets of glass, others in a more conventional manner on flat sheets. Viewing a selection of these is an experience similar to that of visiting a curious museum where objects from an unimaginable past civilisation, or perhaps an alien world, are offered in glass cases accompanied by gnomic inscriptions. A characteristic of Bednarczyk's work is the incorporation of hand-drawn writing full of exuberant flourishes which approaches the indecipherable, adding a further layer of mystery.

The artist's sensitivity to the power of words infuses his imagery also. The titles of his work speak of angels and heroes without coyness, or the use of words simply for themselves. They hint at the sources of his creativity, of a world in which everything is entirely clear and coherent with everything else. What the viewer is faced with is, however, essentially a mystery with hints of great and important depths awaiting revelation. This poetic rather than literal approach to naming his works is crucial to Bednarczyk, expressing his highly personal and intensely poetic vision of a world that straddles the imagination and hard reality. He chooses this means to illuminate the recesses of his inspiration rather than using a blunter nomenclature, and it may be seen as being central to his manipulation of visual images. When he speaks of angels and heroes one cannot be sure of their origin, and in a sense it does not matter. What one is left with is a haunting series of images that are every bit as real as topographical renditions of real landscape. In Bednarczyk's case the landscape is an interior one that contains its own references to and interpretations of a world that is very real indeed. His works are the product of an artist who approaches his ideas and their implementation with absolute integrity. They are full of potency but do not allow themselves to be deciphered with ease: instead, they require that the viewer should enter into a state of complicity with them, to engage them openly, following which certain meanings might emerge over a period of time.

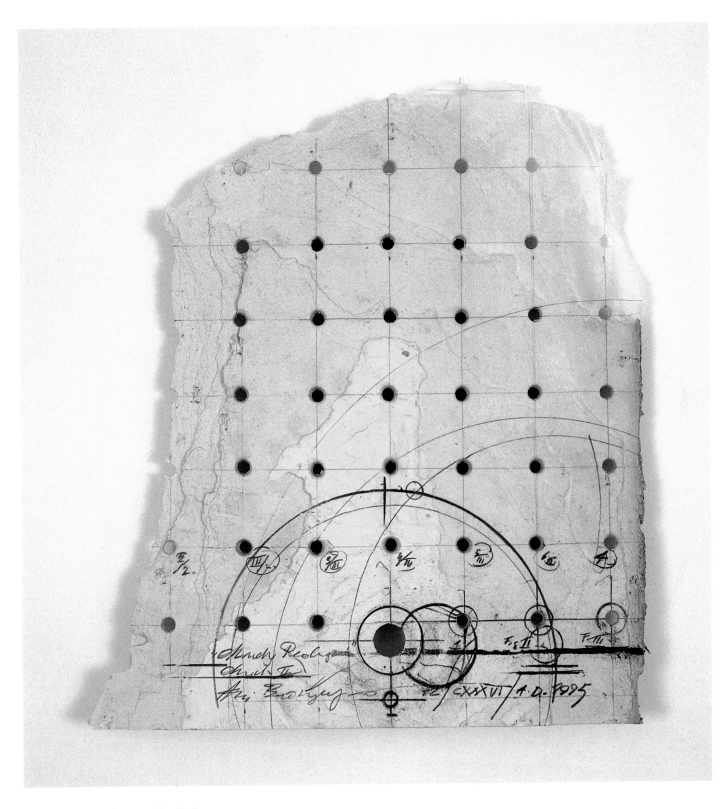

Andrzej Bednarczyk **Scraps of Reality II**
1995, Own technique, 43 x 38 cm. Collection of the artist

Andrzej Bednarczyk **Painted Heroes IV**
1992, Own technique, 70 x 100 cm. Collection of the artist

Andrzej Bednarczyk **Anatomy of Angels Vol IV**
1996, Own technique, 26 x 93.5 cm. Collection of the artist

Grzegorz **Bednarski**

Grzegorz Bednarski was born in Bydgoszcz in 1954 and graduated from the painting studio of Professor Jan Sczancenbach at the Krakow Academy of Fine Arts, where he studied from 1975–80 and where he now teaches. He lives in Krakow and pursues his work in painting and drawing. The central motif of his work for many years was the spiritual dimension of the human condition expressed in a style both figurative and close to expressionism. It was not, however, merely a response to the social and political conditions of Poland in the years following his graduation that led him to elect to follow such a form. The early 1980s presented many difficulties to the Poles and to artists in particular. Deprived for a time of the possibilities of showing in the former establishment system of galleries they sought alternative spaces, among them the temporary 'gallery' spaces of churches where much art was shown that would have been considered unacceptably confrontational had it been shown under any aegis other than that of the Church.

The alignment with what were considered to be 'spiritually clean' spaces gave a fresh impetus to much Polish art of the period and the powerful means offered by forms of expressionism proved attractive to many young artists of Bednarski's generation. While some such artists have with the change in circumstances moved on from that alignment and style, Bednarski has maintained connections with them. His style remains loosely expressionist but has undergone a process of evolution. He willingly admits the influence of Baroque painting, of Spanish artists in particular, and a fascination with Spanish mysticism with its concept of 'dark light'. Drawn to the subtle nuances of light that appear in the painting of the 18th century, as well as its precedents in the art of other eras, he has sought his own means of portraying this in his paintings. In an extended series of paintings and drawings, as well as works in pastel, under the general title 'The House of Misterium', from 1989 onwards he showed human figures, whole or mutilated, enclosed within the confines of red cells. These images related to the Biblical Passion, to torture and the gross inhumanity that has characterised so many of the conflicts of this century, but also to the inescapable suffering brought about by the conflicts in the human mind.

Deeply disturbing though this subject matter is Bednarski nonetheless found it possible to create images that were highly personal and at the same time not without hope. He never allowed the imagery of these works to lapse into a state of despair: there was always, in the act of facing such images and expressing them so clearly, the hope of redemption. In his paintings of the past few years he has moved to the still life as his chosen form and in so doing has turned towards a different and clearer light, that which illuminates everyday objects such as fruit and vegetables, a hat or a knife on a plate. At the same time he has produced a series of pastel drawings of heads — not the desperate decapitated forms of his earlier work but noble sculptural heads suggestive of great wisdom, caught in fugitive beams of pure light. While this work is, superficially at least, simpler, he does not consider it to be a lesser form, and has written (in 1995) that 'an ordinary still-life or landscape may convey as much as a "screaming" painting'.[1]

The drawings shown here date from 1992, around the time at which Bednarski's art changed direction. As with his work in painting, they are much concerned with the nature of light and with humanity. He uses line with great care — either open, as in the case of *Blind Man*, or closed in with areas of crosshatched tone, as in the other two drawings shown. The modulation of light has informed all his work, as has a strong sense of composition. These two elements are never incidental, and in these drawings become crucial elements without which there would be little sense. They offer a direct route to understanding Bednarski's working methods and his art in general for, deprived of the layers of manipulation that come of necessity with the techniques for applying colour, it is possible to see the underlying structure of his inspiration and work. That his work has integrity and strength is without question and the elemental nature of the drawings shown prove that Bednarski, far from settling into a safe means of expression, is an artist whose exploration of the nature of life is far from over.

1. 'Ordinary Little Pictures', text by Grzegorz Bednarski in the catalogue of his exhibition at the Galeria Kordegarda, Warsaw, 1995.

Grzegorz Bednarski **Blind Man**
1992, Drawing, 24 x 30 cm. Collection of Anna and Robert Wolak. Photograph: Pawel Chawinski

Grzegorz Bednarski **26, 29, 30, I**
1992, Drawing, 36 x 56.5 cm. Collection: Print Room of the Polish Academy of Sciences, Krakow. Photograph: Pawel Chawinski

Grzegorz Bednarski **X/92**
1992, Drawing, 32.5 x 46 cm. Collection: Print Room of the Polish Academy of Sciences, Krakow. Photograph: Pawel Chawinski

Jozef **Budka**

Jozef Budka was born in Czechowice-Dziedzice in 1953 and lives in Katowice where he studied at the Krakow Academy of Fine Arts' Department of Graphics in that town. He graduated in 1978 and since then has been a member of the teaching staff in the Department of Graphics of the Academy in Krakow. His personal work encompasses painting and drawing as well as printmaking. He has exhibited widely in Poland and internationally, including in Portugal, Germany, Finland, France and the Czech Republic, where he had a successful individual exhibition at the Polish Institute in Prague.

It is significant that Budka and other artists living in the Katowice area have chosen to address themselves to the deeper implications and nature of the place in which they live. Katowice is the main centre of a conurbation with a population of two million (the largest concentration of people in Poland), heavily industrialised and the source of dreadful pollution, the levels of which are among the worst in Europe. The environmental disaster of this area affects the surrounding country, including Krakow, which is 70 km to the east. Katowice is part of Silesia, the large region that stretches to the German border and runs along the mountains of the Czech border, and which has played an important part in the country's history. The twin legacies of history, evidenced by the numerous examples of fine architecture, and industrialisation have both left their mark on the region that also contains some of the finest natural landscape in Poland. That art should flourish as it does in this region is due partly to the undoubted sources of inspiration that come from the natural and man-made environment of the area and partly to the Poles' extraordinary resilience to the chain of historical upheavals that has been the basis of much of their cultural achievement over the centuries. Katowice in the east of Silesia and Wroclaw in the west are now both major contributors to the richness of contemporary Polish visual art.

Budka's work in printmaking, like many of his contemporaries, is innovative in both the techniques that he uses (lithography is a major form for him, but he also has developed a personal approach in which the limitations are extended) and in his choice of subject matter. Nominally figurative, his work is derived from sources closer to literature and psychology than they are to direct transpositions of perceived reality. Towers set in landscape figure prominently, not as an architectural record but as deeper symbolic structures. In one lithograph, *Silence*, 1989 (illustrated), the top of a massive ornate tower is seen, from the top of which a head emerges, exploding into fragments. In the background can been seen the sunlit towers and domes of some imaginary city, the evidence of a highly structured civilisation. In the foreground all is confusion, any detail obliterated by scrubbed in areas of tone. In another lithograph, *Tower of Illusion*, 1991 (also illustrated), there is a similar arrangement of forms, but in this case the tower is less decorated, more of a fortification than an essay in architectural style, and the background is less distinct. In one catalogue a reproduction of this work is accompanied by a quotation from Umberto Eco's novel *The Name of the Rose*, in which the themes of architectural and philosophical folly are worked out in a vast castle which is in the end destroyed in the search for truth. Seen in terms of the recent evolution of Poland, as well as in the longer historical context of the country, the symbolism of these two prints has a potency that is undeniable, in that the creation of the new comes from both a knowledge of the truth and an awareness of the need for the destruction of the falseness of past structures.

However, not all of Budka's work is concerned with architecture. In a series of prints titled 'Wulkan' ('Volcano'), one of which is illustrated, the theme is more mysterious. Two nude women with attenuated necks, blank eyes and huge hats face each other across an erupting volcano that is reminiscent of the Mount Fuji prints of Hokusai. The insolence of their posture and gesture might be seen as indicating the indifference of elegance in the face of destruction, symptomatic of a society whose evolution from totalitarianism to free-market capitalism carries with it the dangers inherent in the rapid adoption of new ways. In exploring this dichotomy Jozef Budka is an accomplished artist who is seeking innovative means for describing the changing world in which he lives.

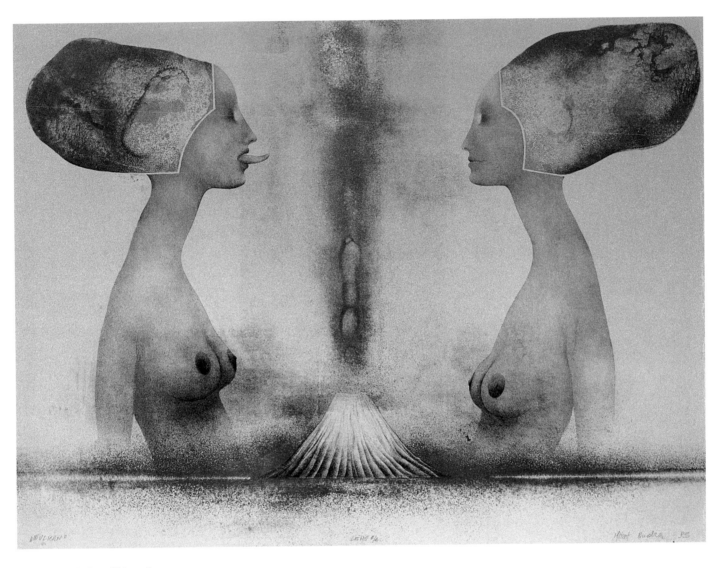

Jozef Budka **Wulkan (Volcano)**
1993, Lithograph, 77 x 57 cm. Collection of the artist

Jozef Budka **Silence**
1990, Lithograph, 53.5 x 49.0 cm. Collection of the artist

Teresa Bujnowska **Seven** (from the 'Manifestion of Numbers' series)
1994, Drawing, distemper on paper, 62 x 62 cm. Collection of the artist

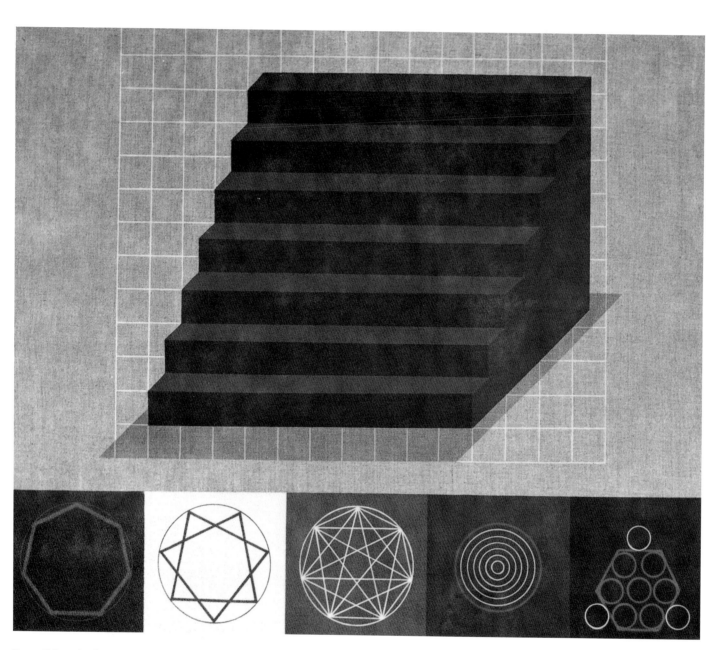

Teresa Bujnowska **Construction Seven** (from the 'Tetraktys' series)
1994, Drawing, acrylic on canvas, 55 x 65 cm. Collection of the artist

Teresa Bujnowska **Ideogram XX** (from the 'Ideograms' series)
1994, Drawing, photo, acrylic on paper, 74 x 52 cm. Collection of the artist

Halina Cader

Halina Cader works in drawing, painting and photography. She was born in Krakow in 1952 and studied at the Academy of Fine Arts in that city, graduating from the Graphic Art studio of Professor Mieczyslaw Wejman in 1976. She currently teaches at the Pedagogical College in Krakow and bases her work on the immediate environment in which she finds herself. In restricting herself to her immediate experience of the city in which she lives Cader is not limiting the possibilities for her art: instead, it gives her a tightly focused perspective and enables a concentration on the essentials of this aspect of her visual experience. Krakow provides a contradiction in cultures and the environment that contains them in that the historic core, with its long tradition of high cultural enterprise, is surrounded by post-war industrial buildings and the concrete suburbs that sprang up to house the workers in them. The conflict between the two cultures, while not antagonistic, has had a profound effect on the post-war generations of artists, giving them a context very much changed from that which nurtured the vitality of the pre-war avant-garde in the city.

Cader's position as an artist within Krakow's cultural life gives her one viewpoint while her chosen working context gives her another. If there is a conflict in this it is not clearly discernible in her work which is carefully created over a considerable time, resulting in cool constructed planes and tones that delineate her response to the buildings she encounters on a daily basis. She has adopted the series as a major means in her work over the past twenty years, allowing her to produce an extended response not possible within a single image. From 1978–88 she worked on 'Collection No. 2', 'Bridges' and 'Pavillons' which comprise monochromatic pencil drawings on grey paper and xerographic copies, all based on photographs of buildings. While she has abandoned xerography as a medium since 1990, the experience of working on these series gave her a developing skill in the use of tone which she continues to put to good effect in her newer work.

In 1990 she began a new series of diptychs with the title 'Entres', based on carefully composed images of sections of buildings where planes and surfaces intersect to give complex variations in tone and texture. These works were completed using crayon, pencil and tempera on grey and black paper and give the slightly paradoxical appearance of being mechanical while at the same time obviously being the result of a lengthy period of absorption in the application of the chosen materials. In this they reflect the nature of the buildings themselves — hard concrete, steel and glass structures designed to criteria very different from those of the buildings in the city's historic centre. However, both types of buildings contain all that is organic in the processes of daily human life, but to different levels of satisfaction of people's needs. In 1994 Cader began two new series of work, working in diptych and triptych form using drawings on canvas or photosensitive canvas. Entitled 'New Pavillons' and 'Tram Stop Boys', the first continues the theme of 'Entres' while the second continues her work in creating an ongoing series of photographic portraits of teenage boys from the suburbs of the city.

In the 'New Pavillons' series she is extending her approach to interpreting buildings: each diptych has one part in which the structures of buildings are investigated to expose the tonal complexity of their surfaces and the play of light, shadow and reflections on their textures, the other part being a more abstract treatment of that light using paint, tending towards the subversion of the original theme. The combination indicates a move towards a looser approach which shows signs of further development in future and which may well lead to a new direction.

Like a number of others of her generation, Cader has chosen to work almost exclusively in monochrome. Whether this is a reaction to the tradition of Colourism that has characterised so much Krakow painting in the past, or whether it is a response to the sense of alienation that came about during the upheavals of the 1980s is uncertain. It does, however, represent a thread in the complexity of recent Polish graphic art which illuminates well the social and cultural evolution of the country. In addition, the finely executed work of Halina Cader offers a view of one of Europe's most fascinating cities that is very different from that usually seen by visitors, and as such warrants close consideration.

Halina Cader **Entres VII / VIII (Diptych)**
1992, Drawing, crayon, ecoline on paper, each 50 x 56 cm. Collection of the artist

Halina Cader **Entres I (part 1 of Diptych)**
1990, Drawing, pastel, tempera on paper, 50 x 65 cm. Collection of the artist

Halina Cader **Entres I (part 2 of Diptych)**
1990, Drawing, pastel, tempera on paper, 50 x 62 cm. Collection of the artist

Wanda Czelkowska

Wanda Czelkowska is primarily a sculptor, although her sculpture frequently contains drawing as an important element and she also pursues drawing as an autonomous activity. In her work these two approaches form a coherent whole. Born in Brzesc in 1930 she lives and works in Krakow where she studied sculpture at the Academy of Fine Arts from 1949–54. Her work has been shown in individual exhibitions in Poland, France, Austria, Scotland, Holland, Hungary and Germany as well as in over fifty group exhibitions in Poland and Norway. Her approach is essentially that of an artist for whom the normally accepted boundaries do not apply and who seeks through her work to reach for a personal understanding of the nature of creativity and its relationship to human endeavour.

Perhaps the key work in her long career is *Absolute Elimination of Sculpture as the Conception of Shape*, first made in 1972 but re-created at the Muzeum Sztuki Wspolczesnej in Oronsko in 1995. It consists of sixty-six concrete slabs laid in a grid (15 m x 8 m approximately) on the floor of the gallery, sixty-six electric light bulbs hung in a matching grid on the ceiling and the space between them. The void thus created is that in which the conventional idea of sculpture is signified: it may be imagined, observed from outside the grid as being implied or realised by walking between the two surfaces that are created by the concrete and the light, in which case the occupation of the space suggests something akin to the usual idea of sculpture, but in a transitory manner only. One view of such work is that it is essentially conceptual and devoid of anything but extreme intellectualism. However, in the case of Czelkowska it succeeds in a manner different from much of the Conceptual Art produced in Western Europe and North America in that it invites the personal involvement of the viewer as an active participant within the artist's conception, occupying temporarily the space that thereby attains something of the calm that infuses places that are defined as being spiritual.

Czelkowska is uncompromising in her approach to sculpture, insisting on a rigour that is not as easily accommodated within gallery or exhibition situations as is conventional work in three dimensions. However, her work is now gaining wider acceptance and in 1996 she created *Park Sculpture — Enclosed (the construction exceeding the concrete place of a disinherited orangery)* at the Polish Sculpture Centre in Oronsko. It consists of a construction of spruce beams and iron screws arranged to form 'an infinite straight line through other infinite straight lines' with notional dimensions of 35 m x 10 m x 5.4 m. While this is sculpture in the sense that it is three dimensional it is at the same time a form of drawing within a real space which implies a greater space through the imagined extension of each line formed by the spruce beams. Drawing as a pure element is used as an integral part of another major work, *The Ascension*, 1994, in which square panels bearing swirls of gestural curves in pastel interspersed with blue panels form a two-sided work over 3 metres in height.

In her drawings, examples of which are illustrated here, Czelkowska is concerned with the creation of a greater space within the limited dimensions of the paper. *Anthony's Landscape XII*, 1994, recalls to some extent the drawings of Mondrian and the approach is similar. Curved lines in charcoal and pastel form a dense network of gestures beyond which the white of the paper implies a limitless distance. Whether it is derived from a real landscape or the conception of landscape in the mind is not relevant. *Tree I*, from the mid-1980s, bears the inscription, 'One mustn't give a human face to evil and yet he carries it, evil, within himself'. The tree in this drawing is a mechanised, dehumanised construction: the curves and circles are in the form of a tree, but the organic nature is missing. *My Tree*, 1985, is also composed of lines and circles but the form is looser — it is perhaps the image of a tree as seen when looking upwards to the sky.

In her drawing and in her sculpture Wanda Czelkowska is concerned with the nature of space and equally with the nature of humanity within it. The forms she uses create work that hovers between figuration and abstraction, between certainty and uncertainty, yet they comprise a body of work that marks her as a European artist of considerable distinction whose achievement has yet to be fully recognised within her own country and further afield.

Wanda Czelkowska From the cycle **Anthony's Landscape XII**
1994, Drawing, charcoal, pastel on paper, 103 x 72 cm. Collection of Jan Motyka, Krakow. Photograph: Pawel Chawinski

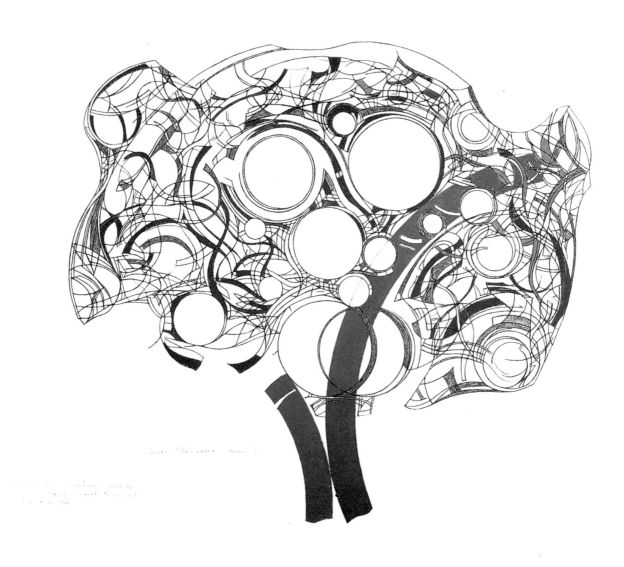

Wanda Czelkowska **Tree I**
1986, Drawing, charcoal, tempera on paper, 70 x 70 cm. Collection of the artist. Photograph: Pawel Chawinski

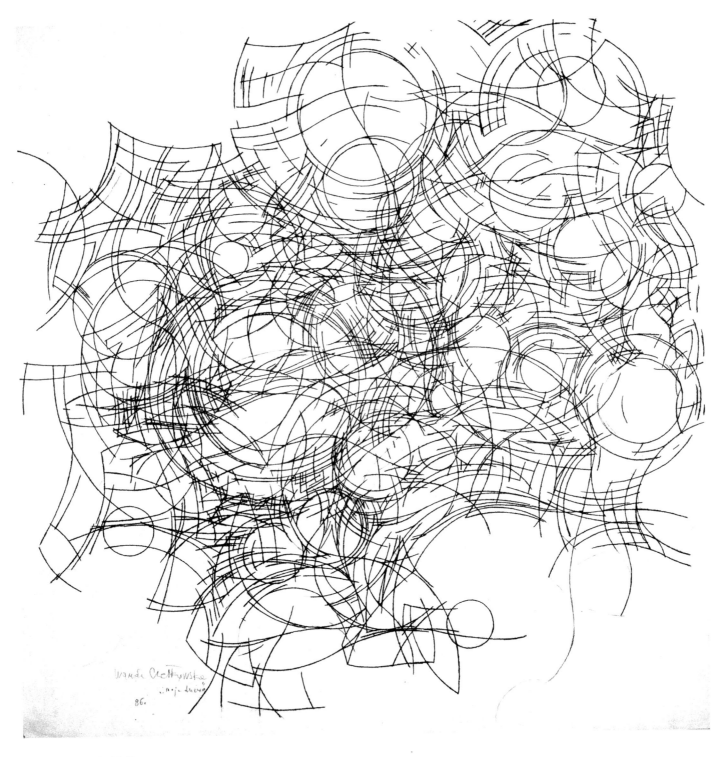

Wanda Czelkowska **My Tree**
1985, Drawing, charcoal, tempera on paper, 70 x 70 cm. Collection of the artist. Photograph: Pawel Chawinski

Jan Dobkowski

Jan Dobkowski's career as an artist is characterised by a consistent and impressive development and has been marked by many successful exhibitions both within Poland and internationally. He was born in Lomza in 1942 and completed his studies in Warsaw, first at the High School of Fine Arts and then at the Academy of Fine Arts, graduating in 1968 from the studios of Juliusz Studnicki and the celebrated Jan Cybis. His work in painting has been entirely consistent with his work in drawing and both have matured together, achieving a high point in recent years.

The underlying lyricism of his work in both line and colour marks him as a sensualist, one deeply in touch equally with the full range of human emotions and the realm of physical experience. The lightness of touch that comes from his work is often underlain with an exuberant eroticism, one which never lapses into prurience but which is consistent with life lived to the full. There is, however, another side to Dobkowski's art, one which reveals his engagement with philosophy and the wider issues of existence. It is clear from a study of his work over the years since his graduation that he has been equally aware of the darker side of life, affirming through his paintings and drawings the dualities of life and death, pleasure and pain, in equal measure. The vitality of his approach, the manner in which he uses colour to describe form and form to describe the energy which creates it has always indicated that he is clearly aware of the fragility of life and through this the urge for celebration of the moment, beyond which nothing can be certain.

His early drawings, those from the late 1960s and through the 1970s, now appear to be limited, trite even, creating overtly sexual images with fine ink lines that portray endless breasts and genitals entwined with tendrils and curlicues that echo the decadence of Art Nouveau. There is an obsession bordering on ferocity in these images, which interestingly occur again in a series of drawings dating from 1993, and they could perhaps be dismissed quite easily were it not for the other work that was done in parallel with them. One can discern his awareness of the eternal nature of the experience that comes from the biological nature of human existence and the potential for new life that is contained within the couplings of male and female. One may also experience his identification with the matter of myth and religion, with their symbolism and systematic structures, a study of which shows that the similarities between apparently opposing constructs are infinitely greater than their differences.

The two series from which the works shown here have been taken can be seen to complement each other. In the 'Uniwersum' series of watercolours, dating from 1992, he extends the work he did in the 'Ocean' series, building up complex structures of lines in colours much more subtle than the strident primaries of his early work. Just as the ocean can be seen in symbolic terms as the place from which life sprang and, in metaphysical terms, in which we live our lives, so the universe contains all that and a great deal more, reaching outwards to the very nature of life itself, to the eternal and spiritual and towards the ultimate question of what it was that preceded us and what it will be that succeeds us — the 'sacrum' is implied. In *Uniwersum XV* the elemental form of the triangle is drawn primarily in lines of soft reds and purples, opposed by the vertical blue striations of the background. Within the triangle swarm tiny black figures, drawn with limbs extended or truncated so that they come to resemble fragments of genetic structure.

In the 'Genesis' series of paintings and drawings Dobkowski has chosen to create a coherent expression of his vision through the incorporation of paintings dating back to the late 1970s, some from previous series, others more individual, with drawings bearing the specific title of the series itself. It appears that he wishes to establish a mid-career point for himself with a summation of the work so far, but remaining open-ended. In an artist of lesser certainty this could be risky but in the case of Jan Dobkowski it achieves some success. He has said of his work that 'Line is a trace of thinking...'. The work of this artist demonstrates with assurance that the thinking continues to evolve and that it has the potential to add to an already considerable body of work.

Jan Dobkowski **Uniwersum XV**
1992, Watercolour on paper, 48 x 63 cm. Collection of the artist

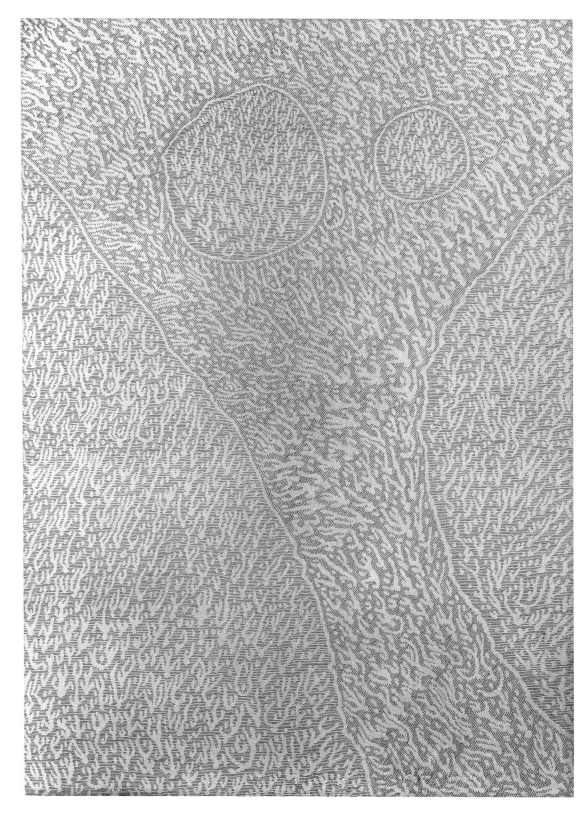

Jan Dobkowski **Genesis CLXXVI**
1996, Drawing on paper, 76 x 56 cm. Collection of the artist

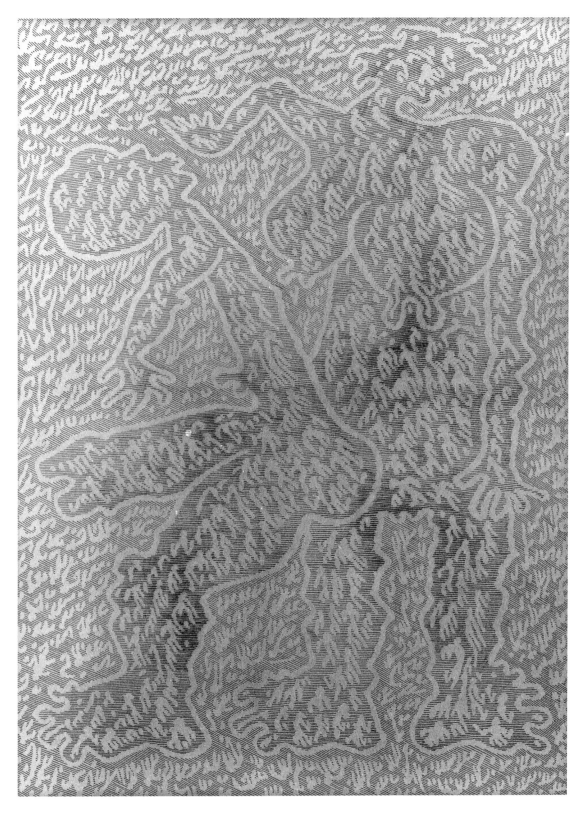

Jan Dobkowski **Genesis CLXXXVII**
1996, Drawing on paper, 76 x 56 cm. Collection of the artist

Agnieszka Dutka

A reaction to urban living provides the basis for Agnieszka Dutka's work in aquatint. She was born in 1959 and educated in Krakow, graduating in 1992 from the Department of Graphic Arts at the Academy of Fine Arts. Living in a city which combines an ancient and beautiful historic centre with less than attractive concrete suburbs sets up tensions that are common in many other cities in the world and which those who live in them resolve in their own ways. Krakow's Academy and the associated artistic milieu of the city have long been the seedbed of artistic invention and development, relying equally on a strong awareness of tradition and a reputation for experimentation. These factors are of primary importance in an analysis and understanding of Dutka's work.

Aquatint is a printmaking method that results primarily in areas of tone rather than the lines that are produced in etching. While difficult to master and requiring considerable skill in the processes involved, it is nonetheless a method that is capable of producing the full range of tones in an infinite series of gradations from pure black to pure white. In adopting this technique for her present series 'Miasto' ('Town'), Dutka has added a limitation to her work, but one that she utilises with growing assurance, as she does in her choice of the basis of a geometric grid, usually of two opposing diagonals but on occasion a vertical axis crossed by a single diagonal. Within this format she develops complex patterns of what appear to be structures with pitched roofs, narrow thoroughfares and enclosed open spaces. These are not depictions of Krakow, or of any other specific city, but rather of the idea of the town as a constructed environment within which the social systems of the community operate.

The human figure does not appear in these prints and indeed there is little to suggest the scale of the environment that is shown. It can be assumed that the scale is small relative to the human form but the acceptance of this assumption in itself creates a sense of unease equal to that of the opposing possibility of the scale being relatively large in human terms. Lacking visual clues, viewers must determine any such reference for themselves. Some works in this numbered series are contained within a rectangle but in others the rectangle is broken by forms that extend beyond it or penetrate it, and in yet others there are sections that have a different scale of structures within them. This variation of the inherent possibilities creates a shifting dynamic within the visual language that is used, setting up further tensions. As examples of skilfully worked applied geometry, this series of prints has a powerful presence that in itself is very satisfying. The real power in Dutka's work lies in her ability to use a deliberately restricted range of means to explore the possibilities of expression of the notion of the town.

The viewpoint is from above, looking obliquely downwards; the light that illuminates these metaphysical places is also oblique, casting shadows in some parts, lighting the planes of some roof slopes and walls in others. This use of chiaroscuro creates a deeply three-dimensional illusion in some works of the series, an effect that is pronounced in those works in which large open spaces are delineated where the strong highlight produces the effect of artificial light that emanates from within the forms of these strange places rather than being cast on them from beyond. Darkness and light are essential elements of the series, values that are independent of any light from outside the places shown. Combined with a lack of figurative reference, these elements create a world that recalls the strange cityscapes of Giorgio de Chirico and also the impression of places from which human life has departed, if it was ever there, or otherwise has not yet come into existence. They are coldly poetic in their integrity: lacking the explicit presence of emotion they convey a sense of alienation, of places in another world where the absence of human discourse and the trivialities of daily life are total.

For all the coldness that these impressions convey it is clear that Agnieszka Dutka has not taken a frozen or unemotional view of the town as a construct, but rather that in her analysis of the human condition of the town-dweller she has chosen to show places in which the possibilities of warmth and community are held in abeyance and not yet made manifest.

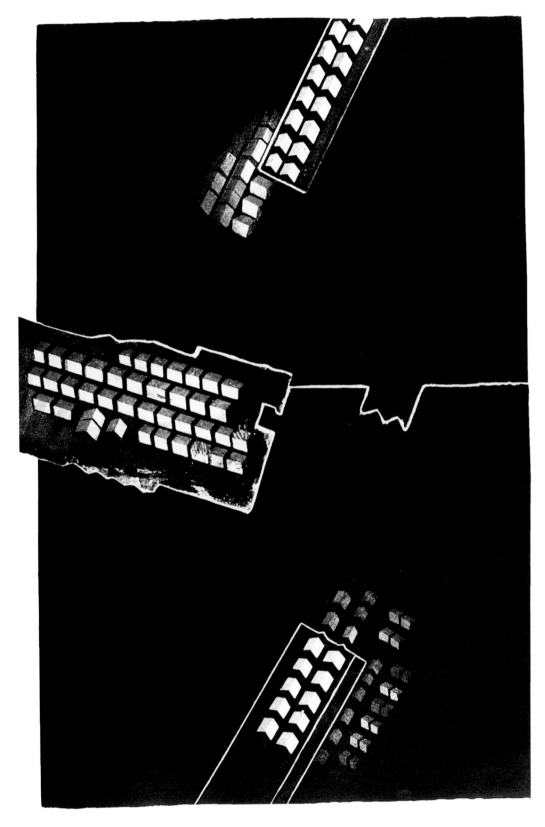

Agnieszka Dutka **Miasto XII (Town XII)**
1995, Aquatint, 94 x 62.5 cm. Collection of the artist

Agnieszka Dutka **Miasto IV (Town IV)**
1991, Aquatint, 49.5 x 64 cm. Collection of the artist

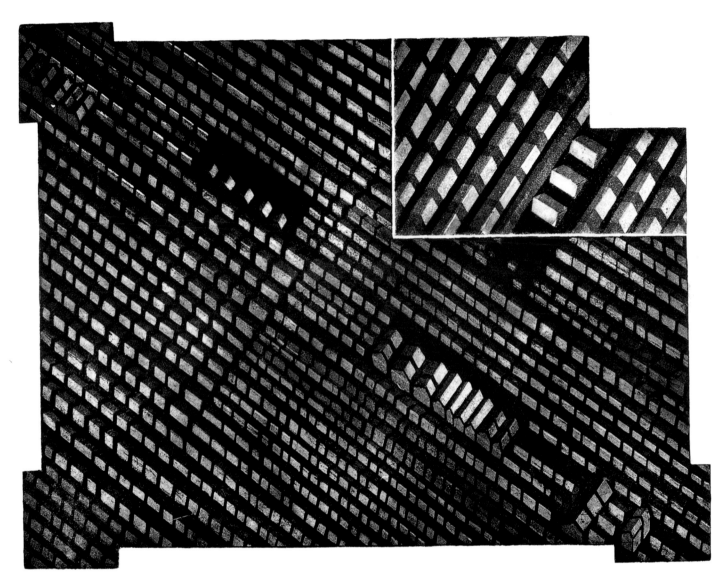

Agnieszka Dutka **Miasto X (Town X)**
1993, Aquatint, 49.5 x 64 cm. Collection of the artist

Stasys Eidrigevicius

Stasys Eidrigevicius was born in a small Lithuanian village in 1943. His father was Polish, his mother Lithuanian, and he grew up in the village where the natural world and the world of folk tales and legends provided the basis for his highly idiosyncratic art. He studied in Lithuania at the Fine Arts Academy in Vilnius from 1968–73, during the course of which he had his first solo exhibition at the Academy's gallery. In 1980 he moved to Warsaw where he now lives and has exhibited extensively throughout the world, achieving considerable success and recognition for his unique work.

It is hard, fortunately, to pin Stasys (by which name he is most recognised) down to any definition, nor would he wish this, as he is active in many fields, including Ex Libris prints, drawing, painting, sculpture, poster art, book illustration, installation and theatre. In all his work he has created a world of his own which is not only entirely coherent but also perfectly believable, a world derived from the mythology that informed his childhood years interwoven with haunting images from his imagination and his reflections on the world in which he lives. His is a gentle vision, untainted by violence or overt politics, in which the innocence of childhood runs clear and pure. However, the threats of the adult world, with all its duplicity and acquisitive desires, is never far beneath the surface of his work, but it is implied rather than stated. His work comes from the true realm of fairy tales in which the innocence of the child, or that of the pure-hearted lover, is the sole hope for salvation in a wicked world and in which good invariably triumphs over evil, light over darkness. The success that he has achieved internationally is due to his ability to work from and refer to commonly understood roots that are independent of any particular cultural framework, touching a deep and common sensibility that is as present in Japan as it is in Europe or the Americas. It seems as if those who experience his work recognise in it elements from their own childhood and transpose it into their own sense of nostalgia for a world and time that seems lost in the pace of contemporary life but which nonetheless still needs to be recognised and is as potent as ever.

This is not to say that this artist's work or world view is light and without substance — the reality is far from this as he achieves a rare depth in his work while still retaining a strong sense of the eternal verities of human existence. Much of his work is based on the form of the mask but it is a mask that reveals rather than conceals, adding complex layers of vitality, character and stillness to the bearer. Masks are much used in his major theatre performance, *Bialy Jelen (White Deer)* in which he tells the story of his childhood and early youth as the events move from the village of his birth, through his schooldays and on to his emergence into the adult world. The white deer of the title refers to the picture that his mother asked him to paint for her, but which he never found time to do while she was alive. In the end he draws the picture and holds it to his face, becoming the white deer of her dreams. The performance is in a mixture of Polish and Lithuanian but its success does not rely on an understanding of the language so much as it does on the need for a recognition of the universal truths that he presents, simply and evocatively, which lie beyond the reach of the spoken word. Much the same can be said of his work in the visual arts which demonstrates not only a firm grasp of the demands of the techniques he uses but also the importance of addressing with accuracy the needs of those who will see the work. There is humour in the work of Stasys that is shy and gentle, but it neither mocks nor condemns, revealing instead a powerful empathy with the comic element of the human condition.

The importance of Stasys' work within the context of Polish graphic art is without question. What renders it unique is the manner in which it is equally relevant elsewhere. Based on an imaginary world in which anything is possible — the weaving of straw into gold, for example — it has a power, a sense of simple joy and an affirmation of life that transcend the limitations of place and time.

Stasys Eidrigevicius Illustration for **Hunry**
1993, Painted mask, photo, life size. (Published by Nord Süd Verlag, Zurich)

Stasys Eidrigevicius Poster for **Boris Godunov**
1987, Drawing with colour. Awarded Grand Prix, Paris 1987. (Published by Teatr Wielki, Lodz, 1987)

Stanislaw Fijalkowski **21 VII 95**
1995, Marker on paper, 15 x 11 cm. Collection of the artist

Jacek **Gaj**

Jacek Gaj was born in Krakow in 1938 and studied there at the Academy of Fine Arts from 1956–62, graduating from the studio of Professor Mieczyslaw Wejman. He has taught at the Academy for many years, becoming a professor in 1992, and practises printmaking and drawing. He pursues his highly individual work in a traditional studio full of the impedimenta of a long artistic life — two venerable presses, shelves of books and prints, sketchbooks and portfolios, and numerous paintings, including several by the celebrated Adam Hoffman. Somewhat reclusive in nature he has produced a notable output of work which offers an important contribution to the artistic history of his native city and which has a profound relevance far beyond it.

In the late 1960s and early 1970s Gaj produced a stunning series of etchings with aquatint based on the novel *Die Blendung*, written by Elias Canetti in Vienna towards the end of the 1920s. His illustrations of the events in this dark novel, in which a scholar is subjected to a series of philistine torments by his huge wife, can be seen to be of influence in much of Gaj's later work. His work is also comparable in feeling with that of Max Beckmann and George Grosz and with the literary and artistic products of the angst-filled world of central Europe. Often grotesque, full of irony and half-familiar faces, it has long been involved with the depiction of the absurdities and the darker side of social intercourse, and also with the intricacies of relationships and the petty cruelties of daily life.

The manner in which Gaj works and the results of long hours of acutely focused labour mark him as a true draughtsman, one who realises fully that such images as he needs to produce are not easily won. He has in the past produced copperplate engravings the quality of which mark him as an heir to the long European tradition in this difficult medium. The process of cutting into the plate with a burin, burnishing and refining the image over and over again until the desired result is obtained is one which has its roots in a time when the craft aspect of such work was highly respected. Although still practised by a few artists it is not a technique which fits happily into the pressure and haste of modern life: it also demands a high level of manual skill and a fine appreciation of the art of drawing. To have produced such a remarkable number of powerful images as Gaj has done is a rare achievement. One such image is *Odysseus for B*, 1969, which portrays a psychiatrist friend of Gaj hunched in a small rowing boat amid malevolently curling waves full of faces and grasping hands. It is a powerful image with obviously deep personal relevance, but one which demonstrates to the full Gaj's mastery of the technique as well as his acute conceptual skills. It is a matter for some regret that he has ceased, temporarily one hopes, to work in copper engraving.

For the past few years he has worked solely in drawing, using Indian ink and a selection of pens. His images are exclusively figurative in style, recording the actual or imagined events surrounding a cast of characters, with portraits of his friends and people seen in Krakow, self-portraits (sometimes nude, recalling the Canetti series, sometimes as the artist drawing), people peering through windows, curious symbioses, multiple hands suggesting restless movement, strange incidents, and strange coincidences of objects, tangled together or isolated — in fact the whole gamut of urban life. Often untitled (one senses that titles would in any case be extraneous) they show a world that operates entirely according to its own logic and which at the same time borders on the absurd world of the plays of Ionescu — the logic of the illogical. Gaj is not afraid to portray the alienation of the modern world and does so with verve and aplomb. His creative power as a draughtsman is undimmed and he offers the viewer privileged glimpses of his own very private world and an insight into his persuasive creative mind.

Drawing, as practised by Jacek Gaj, achieves considerable power and the potential to both entertain and to provoke consideration of the manner in which the visual arts can transcend the power of literature. There is no need for translation — these images of a very personal view of Poland communicate with all the directness and precision of the scalpel.

Jacek Gaj **Untitled**
1996, Drawing, pen, ink on paper, 29.5 x 24 cm. Collection of the artist

Jacek Gaj **Untitled**
1995, Drawing, pen, ink on paper, 24 x 28.5 cm. Collection of the artist

Jacek Gaj **Untitled**
1991, Drawing, pen, ink, brush on paper. Collection of the artist

Barbara **Gawdzik-Brzozowska**

The career of Barbara Gawdzik-Brzozowska has involved her in many areas of the applied arts but it is drawing which has remained central to her personal artistic life. She was born in Katowice in 1927, moving to Krakow in 1939 where she lived until moving to Zakopane in 1959 with her late husband, the celebrated painter and teacher Tadeusz Brzozowski. During the German occupation of Poland in the Second World War, when formal art education was all but unavailable, she studied drawing under Jerzy Fedkowicz at the School of Tailoring, then followed this with studies at the revived Krakow Academy of Fine Arts from 1945–52, completing her studies in painting under Eugeniusz Eibisch and gaining her degree in graphics under the supervision of Konrad Srzednicki. During her studies she began producing illustrations for periodicals and books, including many books for children, work that she continued until the mid-1970s. She was also involved in designs for a number of institutions such as the Museum of Auschwitz, mural painting for a number of churches, fashion and accessory design, interiors for hotels and work with the Jankowski group of architects, who gained first prize for the Polish Pavilion at Expo '68 in Bruxelles. She gave up her work in applied arts in the late 1960s to concentrate on her drawing, and since then she has exhibited widely, gaining recognition and a number of awards. Her work is now included in the collections of many museums and galleries in Poland and other countries.

Drawing for Gawdzik-Brzozowska is an exacting art, requiring delicacy of touch as well as an intimate knowledge of the materials she uses — mostly pen and ink with the addition of watercolour or colour pencil. The resulting lightness that she achieves has given her work an instantly recognisable style, one based on a mixture of the exotic and the humorous. She does not, however, simply produce 'funny' drawings — there is always the sense of an underlying seriousness, bordering on the sinister at times. Much of her work is in the form of portrait, based perhaps *on* those she knows but never *of* them, more usually from the realm of imagination. The characters she portrays occupy a strange world: they are never shown with the context of a background, and most works are of head and shoulders only, frequently in profile. Within these limitations the artist has created a growing cast of characters that could be from some arcane drama. There are echoes of the characters in the writings of Mervyn Peake or the 'magical realists', whose identity is bounded by the incredible worlds of the imagination that they occupy.

Most of the characters she draws are women, cats or fish. They occupy a timeless world of luxury and detachment from reality. Purely imaginary, they bear with them hints of their lives, a sense of decadence that does not seem to trouble them. Many wear elaborate hats decorated with feathers or flowers, they have elegantly coiffed hair, earrings, jewellery or ribbons round their necks, gloves on their hands, their mouths are closed but their eyes are drawn wide open and seemingly fully aware of the strange worlds they inhabit. Sometimes they hold cats, sometimes their faces and heads are bound with ribbon and their clothes are held by long threatening pins, and on occasions they are accompanied by small creatures such as a mouse or a cricket. Their stories are untold, they are silent witnesses to something that is unspoken, their dreams — if they have them — remain unrecounted and mysterious.

Detached from any relationship to a known world and lacking any context of their own outside their portraits, the characters in Gawdzik-Brzozowska's drawings intrude into the world we occupy. They create a sense of unease beyond the smile raised at first seeing them, they question by their presence the nature of the reality of the world we occupy. When shown full length with massive and extraordinary hairstyles, bare-breasted and wearing voluminous petticoats, they are reminiscent of the aristocrats of the last days before a revolution, their languorous postures those of the calm before the storm. In the drawings of cats and fish, their eyes strangely and worryingly human, there are echoes of the other characters, but it is perhaps these animals that are most in control of their imaginary lives. Barbara Gawdzik-Brzozowska's art is unlike any other produced in Poland. In its depiction of an entirely 'other' world there is, however, the convincing construction of a society that operates according to its own logic, the reverse of that in the world in which it is made.

Barbara Gawdzik-Brzozowska **Pamela**
1992, Drawing, pen, ink, colour pencil on paper. Collection of the artist

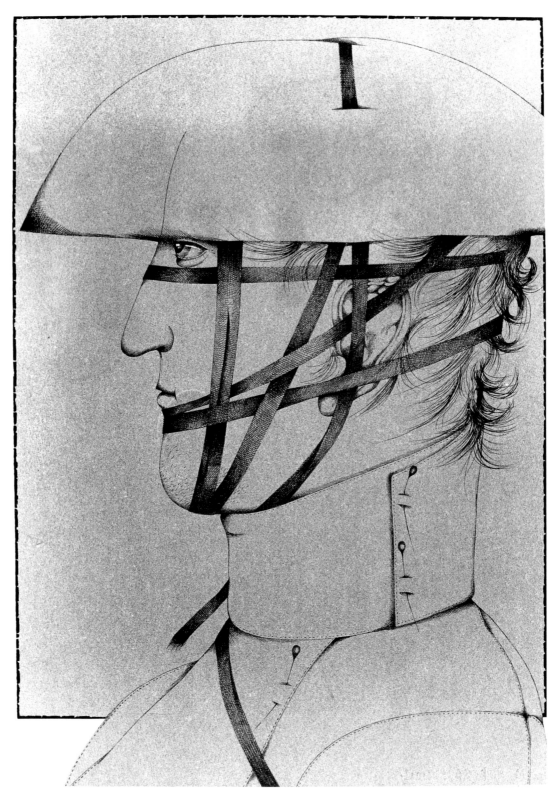

Barbara Gawdzik-Brzozowska **Leon**
1989, Drawing, pen, ink on paper. Collection of the artist

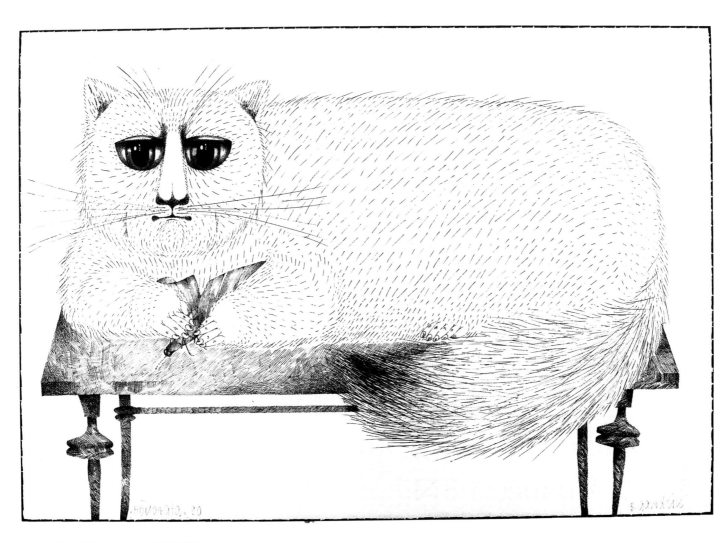

Barbara Gawdzik-Brzozowska **Honorata**
1990, Drawing, pen, ink on paper. Collection of the artist

Ryszard Gieryszewski

Born in Warsaw in 1936, Ryszard Gieryszewski studied at the Academy of Fine Arts in that city from 1959–64, graduating from the Department of Painting and Graphic Arts. He has exhibited widely throughout Poland and internationally, being the recipient of numerous awards, and is a member of XYLON, the International Society of Wood Engravers that is based at Winterthur in Switzerland. He lives in Warsaw and works in relief printing and woodcut.

The basis for Gieryszewski's art is the rectangular geometric grid, and in this there could perhaps be seen a relationship with the work of Mondrian and the theories of the De Stijl group. However, such a comparison is inaccurate as this artist proceeds in a direction that is very different, largely as a result of his use of the third dimension that the techniques of both woodcut and relief printing bring. Thus it is that, far from the flat forms produced in the style of De Stijl, his work defines a real sense of depth. In turn, this allows the fall of changing light to modulate the appearance of the surface, bringing further implications to the carefully controlled composition of his works. Additionally, the artist has introduced subtle organic forms into his work, although they are not always apparent at first. The relationship that comes from this balance between the geometric and the organic adds a rich complexity to his work, provoking a deeper range of possibilities of intent and meaning.

Until comparatively recently Gieryszewski worked exclusively in monochrome, based on pure black and white. This gave a rigour to his prints that allowed for a consideration of the form and composition unhindered by the additional relevance of colour, although the nature of high relief provides areas of shadow that add tonal variation to the surface. In his works, the marks of the relief, derived from the matrix, include forms reminiscent of primitive depictions of the human form or fragments of organic matter. Gieryszewski also incorporates renditions of finger prints (using one such print on his visiting card), those signs of the uniqueness of human identity. One is put in mind of the 'signature' of the hand prints that are seen in cave paintings dating back 30,000 years or more. Also used are Braille symbols, extending further the nature of Gieryszewski's intent in making these prints. They are clearly evidence of his need to utilise his art as a form of communication which does not rely on the written word.

The respected Polish critic Stanislaw Stopczyk, writing about Gieryszewski, described how the artist some years ago told him that 'he had difficulty in communicating with the world and other people' and that 'he wanted to open up contact with the means at his disposal'. Stopczyk recounted how he watched the city's evening panorama with the artist who remarked that the 'ant-hill' building in the foreground, with its haphazardly illuminated windows, contained 'the contradiction between the awareness of human life pulsating there and the sheer impossibility to recognise it'. This sense of urban alienation is a recurrent theme in late-20th-century art and manifests itself in many different ways. In the case of this artist the manifestation is characterised by a strict control of his chosen forms and the sense of implied reluctance to make specific statements through words that comes from his decision to use a coded form of communication. The resulting prints combine quietness and strength with an unequivocal assurance in the techniques he uses.

In his recent work Ryszard Gieryszewski has incorporated chromatic richness, sometimes in a restrained way with a single colour, as in *12 Kwadratow*, 1995 (illustrated here in black and white), with the addition of a subtly graduated rose pink beneath the central black form, and sometimes, as in *Podzial linie 2*, 1994 (illustrated in colour), in a more emphatic manner. The appearance of colour in the artist's means of communication suggests an interesting development, an additional confidence which is perhaps allied to the changes within his country. The richness given by colour adds an immediacy in a world in which strong colours have come to dominate in the urban environment. However, this does not mean that his earlier work recedes in importance by comparison as there is a powerful coherence in his work over the years. Gieryszewski offers a quiet intensity of vision in his work, one that comes from hermetic roots and is deeply concerned with the role of the artist in society.

Tadeusz Jackowski **Wielkanoc w Sewillii IVB (Holy Night in Seville IVB – Puerta del Perdon)**
1992, Aquatint, 40.5 x 46 cm. Collection of the artist. Photograph: Janusz Kozina

Jerzy **Jedrysiak**

Jerzy Jedrysiak was born in Zakopane in 1954 and studied at the Academy of Fine Arts in Krakow, graduating in 1980 with a diploma for his woodcut and book design projects. He currently lives in Zakopane and is Professor in the Art Department of the Higher Pedagogical College in Krakow where he leads the linocut studio. While many of his generation who graduated at the difficult time of Martial Law and its aftermath in the early 1980s chose to express their reactions to those circumstances through work that was more or less political, or at least critical of the situation, Jedrysiak returned to the roots that had always nourished him, producing a unique contribution to the diversity that characterises Polish graphic art.

Zakopane is a small resort in the Tatra mountains in the south-east of Poland, isolated from the hubbub of metropolitan and industrial Poland, with its own distinct culture that owes more to its mountainous location than it does to the mainstream of the country's culture. The mountains and small villages of the Podhale region have a strong tradition of independence and folk art. The music and decorative arts of the region have long been admired, as has the lush landscape of meadows, forests and clear streams with small settlements of wooden houses and churches. It was this region that was home to Stanislaw Ignacy Witkiewicz ('Witcacy'), one of the most important and visionary Polish artists in the early part of the 20th century. In this idyllic landscape Jedrysiak grew up surrounded by the traditions of the 'górale', the mountain people, with their inventive storytelling, myths, legends and hypnotic music, and it is from these roots that he has developed his art.

Jedrysiak works exclusively in linocut and has produced over sixty editions in this difficult medium, at a uniform size of 65 cm x 50 cm. The technique with which he creates each block is exceptional, with a multitude of lines and delicate details so fine that the resulting prints resemble drawing rather than the work usually seen in the medium. There is a strong sense of narrative in his work, not in the straightforward linear sense of beginning, middle and end, but of a complexity in which everything appears to be happening at once.

He creates a world that has its own crazy logic in which the unexpected becomes commonplace, animals walk upright, strange towers and fish appear in gardens, fully clothed people carry religious banners through the ocean waves and a Concorde aircraft flies across the sea inside a house. In Jedrysiak's prints all these things become perfectly normal and acceptable — the world of the imagination is completely synchronised with that in which we live.

The multitude of references in his work come from a wide range of sources: literary, historic, anecdotal and imaginary. In *Andrew's Sermon to the Birds*, 1989, dedicated to Andrzej Szarek, his sculptor friend from Nowy Sacz, the figure of the late Tadeusz Kantor is shown conducting the waves from a step ladder in full evening dress (this actually happened as a photograph of the event in 1967 shows), while birds nest in the sky, paper boats, a paddle steamer and an old galleon bob about on the waves, and musicians, strange towers and plants emerge from the water to greet the sculptor with his pushchair and its strange cargo. *Macondo*, 1995, is derived from the imagery of the Marquez novel *One Hundred Years of Solitude* and shows a Babel-like construction that turns into a resemblance of an ancient Indian observatory rising from lush vegetation within which a hawk seizes a sailing ship in its talons. Of *In Leendert's Garden*, 1994, which was made for a Dutch friend, the artist writes: 'The time did not exist, we were happy there together. That is how reality interweaves with the dream, the dream becomes real and all this becomes the magic of life'.[1]

Paramount in the work of Jerzy Jedrysiak is the urge to make real, using the best technique he can, the world of his imagination, and through the creation of these images of abundance to produce prints that have a wide appeal. That they are valued as highly by people who wish to make them part of their homes as they are by museums and printmaking festivals throughout the world is a mark of how successful he has been so far. As Jedrysiak says of his prints: 'They contain everything that is important for me, everything that I love. My works are full of magical narrative, where reality becomes a metaphor and fantasy becomes reality'.[2]

1. *Silva Rerum — the Forest of Things*, artist's statement, undated.
2. ibid.

Jerzy Jedrysiak **In Leendert's Garden**
1994, Linocut, 65 x 50 cm. Collection of the artist

Jerzy Jedrysiak **Andrew's Sermon to the Birds**
1989, Linocut, 50 x 65 cm. Collection of the artist

Jerzy Jedrysiak **Macondo**
1995, Linocut, 50 x 65 cm. Collection of the artist

Witold **Kalinski**

itold Kalinski was born in Ornecie in 1949 and studied at the Strzeminski Academy of Fine Arts and Design in Lodz from 1966–72, being awarded his Diploma in Painting and Graphic Art in 1972. He practises painting, graphic art and drawing and lives in Lodz in central Poland.

Painting and printmaking are essentially different processes, requiring that an artist who practises both adopts an individual approach to each medium. The intellectual process from which both originate may be the same but the demands of each medium are such that the final results will probably be very different, even if they are complementary. The characteristic thread in Kalinski's paintings from the mid-1980s is their sense of space: areas of smoothly graduated colour in subtle shades present the wide featureless space occupied by figures, shown either whole or in part, that are themselves smooth skinned and featureless. The dream-like atmosphere of these paintings is cool, cold even, reminiscent of the empty psychic spaces described in some science fiction writing. They are an appropriate response to the conditions that pertained during that period, containing a sense of the alienation that many people in the country felt as Poland entered a period of painful transition.

The treatment of light and dark, conceived in terms of psychological as well as physical dualities, that appeared in these paintings appears also in Kalinski's recent printmaking. Working to a modest, and on occasion small, scale he explores the tensions that result as individuals attempt to come to terms with their positions in society in relation to others and to themselves. He works in linocut, using only black ink and white paper to produce his prints. His figures remain more or less featureless, expressing their tension through the position of their bodies or hands rather than through their faces. They are figures that seem to relate more to a concept of the generalised human condition rather than to specific personal experiences and continue the sense of alienation that is present in his earlier paintings. A print of 1983, *Oko (Eye)* (not illustrated here), shows the head and shoulders of a figure, featureless but for an ear, the hair dissolving into

the white space of the background. The lines of engraving on the figure sweep backwards, echoing the rippling lines of the flag held up to the face by a clenched black hand. A single eye appears in the centre of the flag and acts as a symbol of the thoughts that cannot be guessed at within the anonymous head. It is a silent, joyless and painful image. The image of the eye also appears in *Pielgrzym (Pilgrim)*, 1989, this time within a triangle flying across an empty white background. A figure leans towards the edge of the image, a finger extended, hair streaming upwards in a cone that is echoed by an aggressive cone that rises behind.

The three prints illustrated here continue and develop the themes of Kalinski's work. In *Listopad '90 (November '90)*, 1990, the flags recur, this time shielding the face of the figure who stands, back to the sun, extending a hand gesturing either victory or the cutting motion of the scissors. An additional black hand with clenched fingers appears from the armpit accompanied by a dark shape. The figure turns its back to both the light and the wind, facing perhaps an uncertain future. *Aureola (Nimbus)*, 1992, shows a development in that the whole surface of the print is filled with engraved lines that suggest perhaps a landscape, perhaps a partial figure. Above a curved form, indicating what might be a head, a clear halo is shown, this being echoed by a similar shape around the triangular form held by two hands towards the bottom of the print. The final print shown, *Stychen '95 (January '95)*, 1995, conveys a greater sense of optimism: a figure leans forward winged and haloed in black, reaching into the dark circle. There is nothing to suggest resolution in this print but there is the implication of something approaching hope.

While these are not images that can be comprehended with ease they do represent an important strand in Polish graphic art — that of the manner in which such art can approach the darker side of human experience and respond to it with dignity as well as through the skilful use of a demanding medium. Such art is also an indicator of the degree to which artists can explore the ramifications of change within society as well as the processes of development within the individual.

Witold Kalinski **Stychen '95 (January '95)**
1995, Linocut, 20 x 25 cm. Collection of the artist. Photograph: Zbigniew Kos

Witold Kalinski **Aureola**
1992, Linocut, 51.5 x 41 cm. Collection of the artist. Photograph: Zbigniew Kos

Witold Kalinski **Listopad '90 (November '90)**
1990, Linocut, 56 x 45 cm. Collection of the artist. Photograph: Zbigniew Kos

Andrzej **Kapusta**

ndrzej Kapusta was born in Skawina and studied at the Krakow Academy of Fine Arts, graduating with distinction from the studio of Professor Jan Szancenbach in 1981. Since 1982 he has taught in the painting department at the Academy and lives in Krakow, practising painting, drawing and printmaking. He has exhibited widely and has received numerous prizes and awards.

A number of artists in Krakow, although their work is essentially very different in result, can be allied together loosely under the term figuration in that the source and driving dynamic of their work is the human figure. A wide variation can be seen in the manner of the individual artists' responses to this most ancient of themes in art with each artist following a path that comes from a personal set of references. That Krakow should be the city in which this approach has developed is in part due to the extensive history of art in that city and its close connections with the humanistic culture of the long-established Jagiellonian University. Kapusta is one of the artists for whom the portrayal of the human figure has remained central to his work over a long period.

The content of work in the three mediums he practises is linked, with variations of a number of themes surfacing and receding as his work develops. The nude human figure, drawn in isolation, groups or closely linked pairs, each exhibiting tensions, is one such theme. Standing in poses reminiscent of the classical ideal, crouched or leaning forwards uneasily, or, more recently, in yogic postures — the asanas of Iyengar Yoga — these figures relate to the artist's analysis of the dilemmas facing the individual in society, becoming symbolic as much as illustrative. This can be seen potently demonstrated in his cycle, 'Machismo/Hembrismo' in which the role of contemporary man in society is opened to question. In the 'Ogien i Lod' ('Fire and Ice') cycle of paintings the human form is replaced by geometric forms and these can be interpreted as being conversions of flesh and blood into their equivalent as Platonic solids. Geometric and human forms also occur in the continuing cycle, 'Dobra Energia, Zla Energia' ('Good Energy, Bad Energy'), which adds another dimension to

Kapusta's art. In addition to all these themes must be considered the artist's deep love of music — his studio contains a fascinating collection of unusual instruments.

Kapusta's drawing, as shown here, is a complex and autonomous medium, densely worked, often at a scale as large as his paintings, the two forms complementing each other, not with the former acting merely as a preliminary form for the latter. There is a scale beyond which drawing becomes considerably more than the mere notation of ideas, this scale varying from one artist to another. Other artists may find it possible to achieve the same degree of intensity on a much smaller sheet of paper — in the case of this artist it is evident that he requires sufficient space to enable his ideas to take form and breathe. *Dobra Energia, Zla Energia (Good Energy, Bad Energy)*, 1994, is one of a series of challenging drawings whose origin lies in a print made earlier using a gramophone record as the matrix. Extended into these large-format drawings the idea has achieved a power that was only hinted at in the print. The music is silent and the drawing, worked almost to total black, survives as witness to the energy, whether good or bad one cannot tell, released from the spiral.

The large drawing, *Hembrismo*, is from 1986 but is representative of the series: pairs of figures, all but one pair drawn in profile, stand close, one behind the other, and their gestures are tense — the figures represent a diffuse narrative or form a series of variations of emotional interaction. In *Choral XVI*, 1987, one of a longer series, the areas of tone delineate the fragmented surface of dressed stone, a memorial perhaps of a remnant of ancient architecture, upon which can barely be discerned the traces of figures, almost as in the sense of palimpsest. At the same time the compositional force of the drawing is reminiscent of abstract expressionism, but this is subverted by the addition of the figures at the bottom. The music implied is liturgical chant, but the silence of the drawn stone defeats the implication, leaving only the consideration of the passing of time. In these drawings Andrzej Kapusta succeeds in harnessing the fleeting nature of music or human relationships in time for deeper consideration.

Andrzej Kapusta **Dobra Energia, Zla Energia (Good Energy, Bad Energy)**
1994, Drawing, 100 x 140 cm. Collection of the artist

Andrzej Kapusta **Choral XVI**
1987, Drawing, 100 x 70 cm. Collection of the artist

Andrzej Kapusta **Hembrismo**
1986, Drawing, 70 x 200 cm. Collection of the artist

Jaroslaw Kawiorski

Jaroslaw Kawiorski is another member of the younger generation of Krakow artists whose work is based on figuration. He was born in 1955 and studied at the Krakow Academy of Fine Arts, achieving his diploma in 1980 from the painting studio of Professor Jan Szancenbach. He lives in Krakow and works in painting, drawing and printmaking. As with others who follow associated parallel paths, for Kawiorski each of these mediums, although inter-related, is treated as an essentially autonomous art form. He clearly appreciates that each makes very different demands of the artist and provides alternative means to the same end.

Kawiorski's paintings are more overtly existential in the impact of their underlying philosophy than those of some of his contemporaries, dealing with portrayals of isolated individuals within society, dependent on chance and opportunity in order to relate to others and thereby reach their full potential. The figures are often not fully realised, as if they are still in the process of becoming, but with certain features more clearly defined — a hand perhaps, the eloquent tilt of a head, a querying expression on a face. They relate strongly to the sense of alienation present in late-20th-century urban society, but are not entirely without hope of redemption.

This artist's prints and drawings in ink have a richness which comes from the manner in which use is made of the extreme contrast of black on white, building up densely textured sections in some parts, relying on the fluidity of a single thin line in others to define and modulate the space within the area of the paper. The drawings are mostly sized 100 cm x 70 cm — the scale is an important consideration in this case. While the work relates to an essentially Western tradition of figure drawing there are underlying echoes of the manner in which oriental drawing is made, with the nothingness of the empty areas contributing to the wholeness of the work. Some of the drawings and prints pursue an idea through the depiction of a single form, others through a multiplicity of forms, sometimes very different from each other, sometimes being variations of a theme. Far from suggesting uncertainty on the part of the artist, this manner of working suggests a confidence, tempered perhaps with the understanding of the impossibility of realising fully within a single image the complexity of the origin from which it sprang. Kawiorski knows

well that each work, in whatever medium it is made, cannot ever truly be finished and that the goal of a fully expressed image will always be just out of reach.

This artist's output of work is prolific and the images selected for reproduction offer examples only of the themes he is pursuing. In *Three Figures on a Black Background*, 1996, an etching with drypoint, one figure is inverted, truncated, incomplete, held or tumbling through the blackness; the next two are similar with their heads inclined, facing outwards, one surrounded by blackness, the other by whiteness. In this case which is the negative and which the positive cannot be certain, they are replications or echoes of each other, two sides of the same personality, related yet different. *Head and Labyrinth III*, 1995, is from a cycle which explores both the semantic ramifications of the word labyrinth and the position of this complex form within European culture. Combining two drawings of a head, realised in carefully controlled tonal areas, with sketchy variations on the Cretan Labyrinth, the forms are linked across six thousand years of history. Such is the abiding power of the Cretan myth that a fully resolved explanation is unlikely. It is therefore wholly appropriate that the artist chooses not to seek resolution and prefers to leave the conundrum unanswered. The untitled drawing of 1995 continues this theme, contrasting the two linear drawings in the background and a figure with a fully realised head and scribbled-over body in the foreground. The expression on the face of the female figure contrasts strongly with the corpse-like figures behind, positioning life and death in a potent configuration, the certainty of the one contrasting with the temporal uncertainty of the other.

Jaroslaw Kawiorski is an artist whose sensibilities are fully tuned towards the dilemmas of both contemporary life and the art which springs from it. His competence in the use of his chosen media is undoubted as is his acceptance that completion is rarely, if ever, possible. He is not afraid to work on the dangerous edge of things where the risk of failure is balanced by the equal risk of success and art is, at best, a tentative solution.

Jaroslaw Kawiorski **Untitled**
1995, Drawing, ink on paper, 100 x 70 cm. Collection of the artist

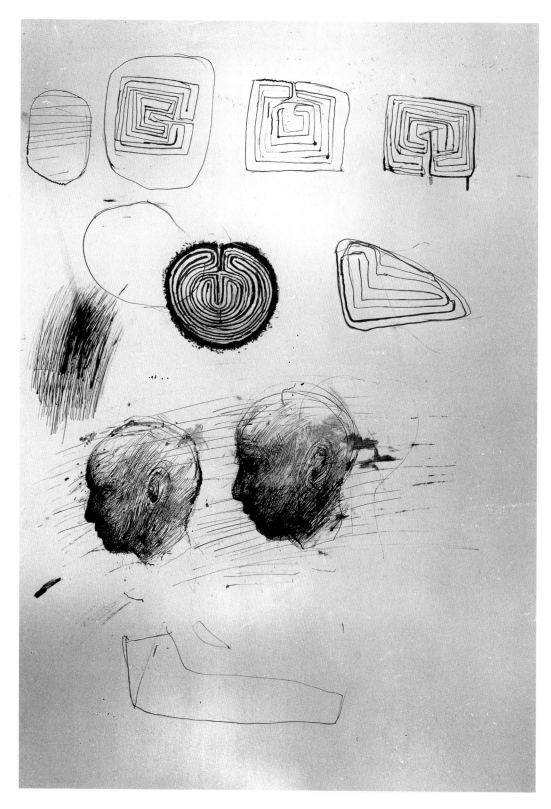

Jaroslaw Kawiorski **Head and Labyrinth III**
1995, Drawing, ink on paper, 100 x 70 cm. Collection of the artist

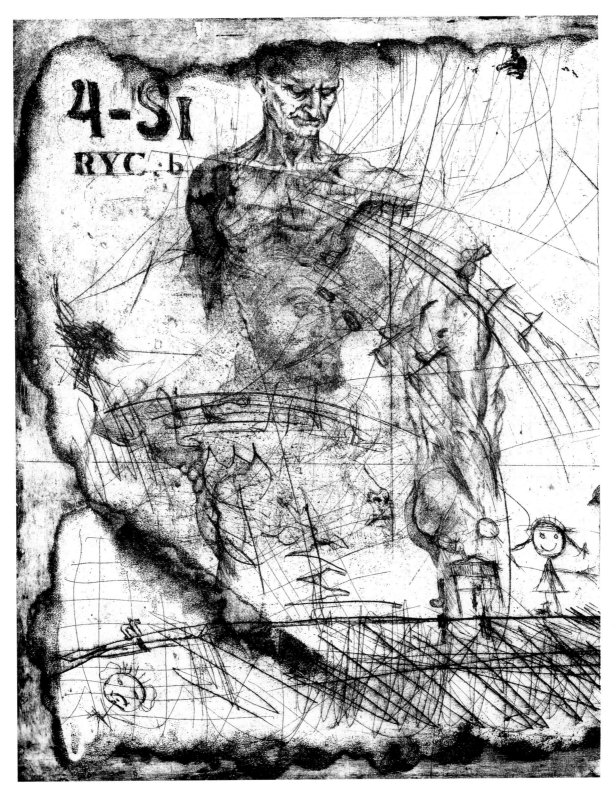

Maria Korusiewicz **Phragment I**
1986, Dryprint, etching, 28 x 37 cm. Collection of the artist

Janina Kraupe

Janina Kraupe is a senior member of Krakow's artistic community. She was born in Sosnowiec in 1921 and studied at the Academy of Fine Arts in Krakow where she is now a professor. Her record of exhibitions since 1948 within Poland and in many other parts of the world is a notable one and her highly individual work has earned her many important awards. She joined the influential Grupa Krakowska in 1958 and was instrumental with it in developing the acceptance of new concepts of contemporary art, the influence of which remain important in the city.

Unusually for an artist at the end of the 20th century, her work is based on a profound knowledge of the esoteric tradition and is closely allied with mystical philosophy. Since 1960 her method of working has been that of 'spontaneous record', in which the result of her thinking on themes connected with music, poetry and magic (in the esoteric sense of the word) is transferred directly into visual form. She also practises astrology, by the traditional method, she insists, not with the use of a computer, and this figures strongly in her work. In addition, she has some aptitude as a medium and telepath. Although this might lead some to take a sceptical view of her art and manner of working, it should be remembered that the Jagiellonian University of Krakow, founded in 1364, claims Nicholas Copernicus among its graduates and has a museum that contains skulls and other wizard's accoutrements said to have been used by the legendary Doctor Faustus. As with other ancient universities, an open-minded view of natural philosophy is long standing. For Kraupe, there is no conflict between the methods of contemporary art she employs and the ancient knowledge that inspires them.

Her work between 1970 and 1980 was concerned with the creation of what she terms pseudo-portraits, cabbalistic signatures and magic texts. The mystical nature of these works and the use made of colour within them ensures that their power of fascination remains and they do not, as much other work of that period, look dated. There is in fact a strong coherence throughout her work which marks it as that of an authentic individual of great artistic integrity. That she uses the symbolic language of magic directly sets her apart from those artists who, consciously or otherwise,

whether influenced by the writings of Jung or not, elect to incorporate some of these symbols into their work. For Kraupe, the validity of the symbols remains paramount. The techniques she employs in her work are primarily those of painting and linocut, in both cases using a full range of colour. The directness of painting differs in essence from the indirectness of linocut in that an intermediate stage — the production of the block — is required. Nonetheless, one senses in her prints the same direct line of creativity that is present in her painting.

Colour for Kraupe, as with the other elements of her work, has a significance that extends well beyond mere chromatic harmony, as each colour is used for its symbolic as well as artistic value. Her Spring 1996 exhibition of linocuts at the Jan Fejkiel Gallery in Krakow demonstrated fully the need for the coherence of all elements in order to make the whole. The works shown here are from that exhibition, which comprised a series of horoscopes, prints based on the symbolic representations of the eight planets, the sun and the moon, and related works. In her introduction to the catalogue she writes: 'Planets, as living beings endowed with character and power, which, through their great personal energy, have always influenced the fates of people, nations and the Earth, have accompanied the development of our culture for thousands of years and contributed to its symbolic and pictorial formation. They have been projections of psychological archetypes connected with the structure of our mind'.

The *Horoscope of Kantor*, 1992, is that of the late Tadeusz Kantor, painter and theatre director, whose work sprang very much from his association with Krakow. It is typical of her work on this theme, containing a full record of his natal chart but also acting as a strong symbolic portrait of the man himself. *Neptune*, 1995, and *Mercury*, 1995, are two of the symbolic portrayals of the planets. The colour in the originals is rich and based on the traditional associations each planet has. The art of Janina Kraupe offers an unusual view of the world, but it is one that richly rewards contemplation, linking the matter of the work itself with the eternal verities of the human quest for understanding.

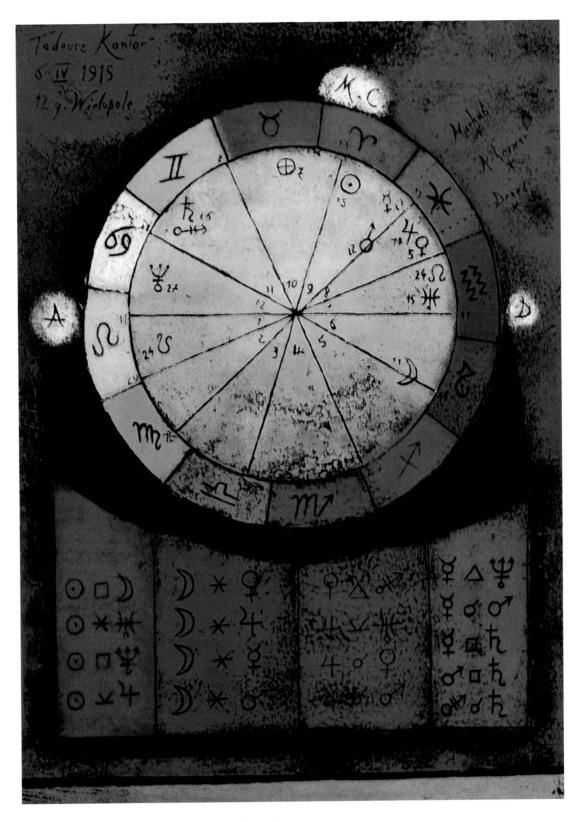

Janina Kraupe **Horoskop Kantora (Horoscope of Kantor)**
1992, Linocut, 61 x 44 cm. Collection of the artist

Janina Kraupe **Merkury (Mercury)**
1995, Linocut, 67 x 47 cm. Collection of the artist

Zbigniew Lutomski **Slad VI (Trace VI)**
1991, Woodcut, 82 x 52 cm. Collection of the artist. Photograph: Adam Wierzba

Zygmunt Magner

Zygmunt Magner is a professor in the Graphics Department of the Academy of Fine Arts in Warsaw whose work encompasses painting as well as drawing and printmaking. He was born in Katowice in 1937, graduated from the Warsaw Academy in 1967 and lives in Warsaw. His work shows a consistent development of form over the years and is closely linked with a deep interest in the nature of time and art. In exploring his own relationship to the present, he has elected since the early 1980s to develop a theme based on the Statue of the Apollo of Tenea, dated to the 6th century BC. In doing so he has established a powerful link between classical Greek civilisation and contemporary Europe, reaching towards the Mediterranean heartland of European culture in order to comprehend more fully the situation at the end of the 20th century. In addition, he allows for a consideration of the nature of artistic creation itself and its relationship to the changing character of society with his intensely detailed and uncompromising work, which lies outside the mainstream of Polish contemporary art or, indeed, that of other countries.

His work in lithography from the early part of the 1970s is typified by heads against dense black or empty white backgrounds that show a progressive disintegration through states of emotional intensity. The ink drawings that were done in parallel with these prints are softer in their impact. For example, *4673* (Magner began titling his work by dates around this time) shows the head of a bird drawn in anatomical detail against the lower belly of a female nude delineated by a skilful cross hatching that is reminiscent of the drawings of Georges Seurat. There is a sense of deep empathy with the human condition in which the head of the bird may represent the spiritual dimension and the body the physical. Other drawings of the period explore aspects of organic form and create an impression of real space within the surface of the paper. As the decade progresses other physical elements appear in the drawings — navels, eyes, nipples, mouths and finally heads and skulls that appear through peeling layers, as if either growing or decomposing.

By the early part of the 1980s the form has all but disappeared. It is significant that in Poland these were the difficult years of Martial Law and its aftermath in which not only artistic creation but also the structure of society itself was opened up to continual questioning. Around 1984 Magner switched his main interest to the statue of Apollo, as this represented for him the concept of the divine absolute through which he found an inspiration which was for him optimistic, bringing him a sense of there being some equilibrium at a time when much else in his country was uncertain. The formalisation of Apollo the Sun God in this statue is presented frontally, arms at the side, the left leg extended. It is in itself a statue that refers back to the figures shown in paintings and sculpture from the high point of Egyptian art, and the concept of art's development over an extended duration of time is introduced. The figure of Apollo is presented in pairs or trios, with each figure drawn so as to recede or advance through the use of chiaroscuro. Through repetition comes added emphasis, through variation the concept of linear time. But Magner's work cannot always be divided into strictly discrete phases as themes interleave. Some drawings from the mid-1980s return to the earlier theme but this time sections of the faces and bodies are overlaid by other structures — grids, rods, crosses and irregular forms. The reappearance is brief but telling.

The drawings from the early 1990s, from which these illustrations are taken, have achieved a monumental scale. Drawing in ink on canvas 250–300 cm high the artist presents the figure of Apollo repeated many times, in rows and columns, some regular, others scattered or turning. One is reminded again of the paintings on tomb ceilings in Egypt where figures are repeated and accompanied by boats and other symbols of the journey into the afterlife. In some of these drawings the figures are fractured or disintegrate into light areas, but in all of them there is a nobility and a profound sense of the potential for art's survival through immense periods of time. Zygmunt Magner is producing work that is as yet little known outside Poland but which has a relevance far wider afield.

Zygmunt Magner **18393 - 1693**
1993, Drawing, pen and ink on canvas, 300 x 150 cm. Collection of the artist

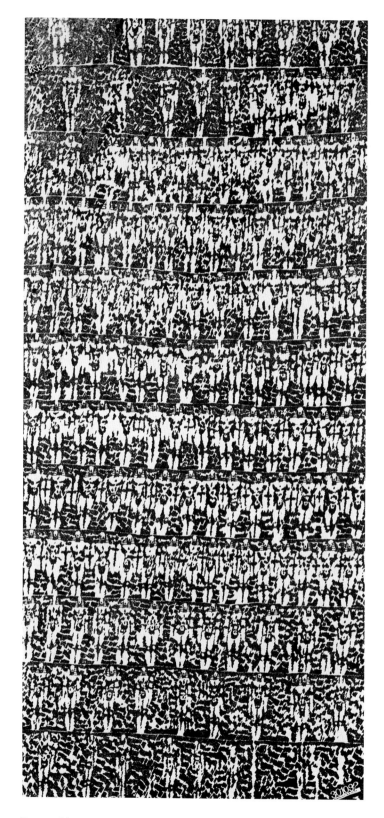

Zygmunt Magner **18992 - 301092**
1992, Drawing, pen and ink on canvas, 300 x 150 cm. Collection of the artist

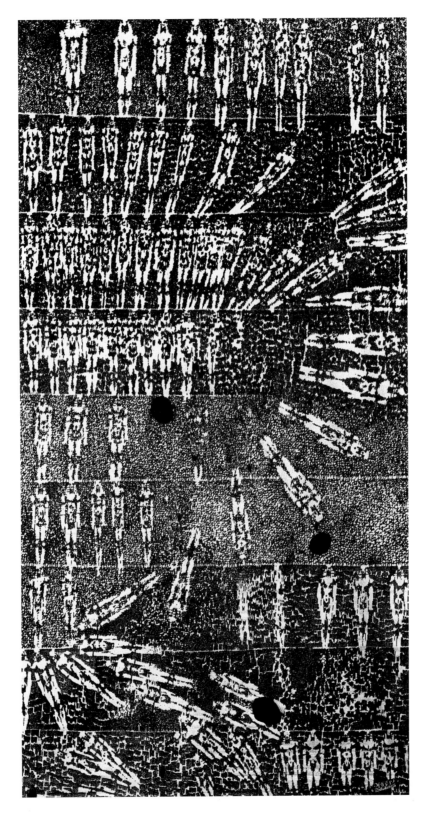

Zygmunt Magner **26692**
1992, Drawing, pen and ink on canvas, 300 x 150 cm. Collection of the artist

Jan Mlodozeniec

Jan Mlodozeniec is one of the elders of Polish poster art whose work over many years has been one of the brightest and most colourful contributions to the visual arts scene in Poland, as well as to the general domestic scene, livening up what was frequently, in the grimmer years, an unrelieved grey environment. He was born in Warsaw in 1929 and studied poster design under Professor Henryk Tomaszewski at the Warsaw Academy of Fine Arts, being awarded his diploma in 1955. That period marks a distinct change in the Polish visual arts, being the time at which the strict insistence of the State that art should follow the Socialist Realist line was relaxed. For poster artists this provided the opportunity to develop forms of expression that were autonomous rather than being merely applied art. For over forty years since then, during the course of which the social and political situation in his country has changed dramatically more than once, Mlodozeniec has followed a consistently successful career as a poster and book designer, cartoonist and illustrator. As one of the leading figures in Polish graphic art, recognised internationally for its excellence, he has produced over three hundred poster designs, has been the recipient of many Polish and international awards, and his work is included in major collections of posters in Warsaw, Poznan, Amsterdam, Prague, Paris and Japan. He has illustrated books by authors as diverse as Steinbeck, Molière and Shakespeare, has had over thirty-four individual exhibitions in Western and Eastern Europe and was given the award for the Best Poster of the Year on no less than eleven occasions between 1965 and 1989.

In the art of Mlodozeniec colour, line, form and lettering (usually hand drawn, a particular characteristic of his work) are fused together in words and pictures to present a coherent whole and an instantly recognisable style. An off-beat humour and gentle satire are used to good effect, not just in his cartoons but also in many of his posters. For example, in a decorative poster from 1974, *Cyrk (Circus),* he painted a clown in clear segments of colour surrounded by thick black lines, the clown having stolen the Y of the title to place it under his arm to use as a catapult. In a simple manner the essence not only of the circus but of the long tradition of the clown is neatly encapsulated. His work in cartoons is equally acute in its powers of observation. That much of this artist's work appears simple and uncomplicated is the result of a finely tuned intelligence coupled with an acute visual sense and an intuitive understanding of the need for all the related elements to be presented as a logical whole. He is expert in his use of materials, fully aware of the technical processes of printing and has in addition a sympathetic sensitivity to the specific requirements of the subjects he illustrates. His skills in the use of hand-crafted techniques set him apart from many of the younger contemporary graphic designers who have come to rely more and more on computer technology: while this can be very effective, it is a reliance that produces work that is cold by comparison with work produced by hand.

Posters must, if they are to be effective, communicate directly and seize the attention of those who see them in as uncomplicated a manner as possible. This requires that the artist must have the ability to distil with accuracy not only the content of the subject in question but also the means chosen for the transmission of that subject. There is in the work of Mlodozeniec a clear sense of the poetic — the reduction of complex emotions and ideas to a bare minimum — and in this he succeeds as few others have. That his father, Stanislaw, was a celebrated poet in the inter-war years is significant, as he gained through him an appreciation of the way in which words operate. He uses lettering playfully, not always abiding by the strict guidelines for classical typography but frequently treating words, and the individual letters of those words, as design elements in their own right, manipulating them to fit in with the overall design. Poland is entering a new and challenging phase in its history in which the role of the poster will take on a different significance. The vitality with which Jan Mlodozeniec approaches his work is shown in the recent examples illustrated here and it is evident that he has lost none of his power, remaining a master of his joyful art.

Jan Mlodozeniec **Arles**
1995, Decorative poster. Collection of the artist

Jan Mlodozeniec **Wiosenny - Salon Plakatu Polskiego (Spring - Polish Poster Salon)**
1990, For Muzeum Plakatu w Wilanowie. Collection of the artist

Marian Nowinski **Dedicated to Leonardo Da Vinci**
1994, Drawing, ink, acrylic on paper, 100 x 70 cm. Collection of the artist

Tadeusz **Nuckowski**

Tadeusz Nuckowski was born in 1948 in Przemysl where he still lives and works as Director of the State Gallery of Contemporary Art. He studied at the Academy of Fine Arts in Krakow from 1969–74, graduating from the wood engraving studio of Professor Franciszek Bunsch and the poster studio of Professor Maciej Markiewicz. He held scholarships from the Polish Ministry of Culture in 1976, 1981 and 1983. He has participated in numerous exhibitions in Poland and internationally, being awarded a number of prizes, as well as having had individual exhibitions in Poland, Norway and Great Britain.

During his time at the Academy in Krakow his work in linocut was severely criticised by some, but he continued to develop it to the point where it is now used as an exemplar of what this challenging medium can achieve. In writing about his own work he tends to be somewhat dismissive and is aware of the problem of fitting his personal creative work into his professional working life. One reason he began working in linocut was that it did not require him to have a studio, such as is necessary for painting. It is a medium that can be accommodated in a small working space and there are indeed historical precedents for this: for example, much oriental printmaking. Perhaps it is not entirely coincidental that there are resemblances between the work Nuckowski produces in a provincial town in the far south-east of Poland, close to the Ukrainian border, and that which comes from the Far East. Indeed, the approach he takes and the results he obtains are comparable with those of artists in the Zen Buddhist tradition. His technique involves drawing directly in ink on the surface of the linoleum block then engraving from the drawing, turning it as he does so into a three-dimensional drawing of negative and positive elements which is then inked before prints are taken by hand, usually on Japanese hoshu or gifu-shoji paper. The artist has written: 'The process is important to me. I mistrust things which come easily and without effort'. Of the results of his work he has said: 'I offer no explanation, since I myself do not anticipate any understanding. I invite you to interpret my work freely'.

Deprived of any intended or imposed anecdotal traces Nuckowski's work simply *is*. Its quiet sense of potency comes from the echoes it creates of other forms — oriental calligraphy, automatic writing, organic traces in rocks, traces of cloud in the sky, eddies in flowing water. His images emphatically do not come from these sources but nonetheless such echoes establish a point of reference beyond which further contemplation of the abstract language of the work is possible. The titles given to the works are not intended to give a clue to their meaning, nor do they succeed in doing so, they are simply a means of identification. The work the artist produced in the mid-1980s is characterised by extensive areas of white (the negative parts of the block) across which are scattered numerous thin lines, scribbles and small areas of dense black. Tensions are created, some are resolved, and the eye is caused to move from place to place within the print. The prints of this period have a greater sense of coherence than earlier work and this move towards definition has continued in the artist's recent work (for example, in *Putative Intention*, 1995, illustrated here). While clearly identifiable forms still do not exist there is a stronger sense of structure and composition.

Around 1994 Nuckowski's work took a fresh direction: as well as continuing to produce prints in the traditional manner he also began experimenting with the way in which they can be manipulated into the third dimension. In the cycle, 'Wiatr w Polu' ('Wind in the Field'), 1994, numerous pyramidal forms printed in densely textured lines overlaid with enigmatic curved lines are placed in a close grid so that the light falling on them modulates the form. This idea is extended with *Wigwam*, an 11cm-high tetrahedron printed in linocut on aluminium foil and photographed in natural grass, as it is in *Ten Small Graphic Objects in Natural Surroundings*, 1996, in which three-dimensional linocuts are photographed arranged on the cast-iron pattern on a drain cover. *Bottle in the Grass*, 1996, illustrated here, extends the idea still further. *Sri Lanka*, 1994 (illustrated), is a unique linocut on Ceylon tea bags, the work of an artist who will doubtless 'not cease from exploration', creating forms of which Tadeusz Nuckowski states: 'If you think so, it's clearly that'.

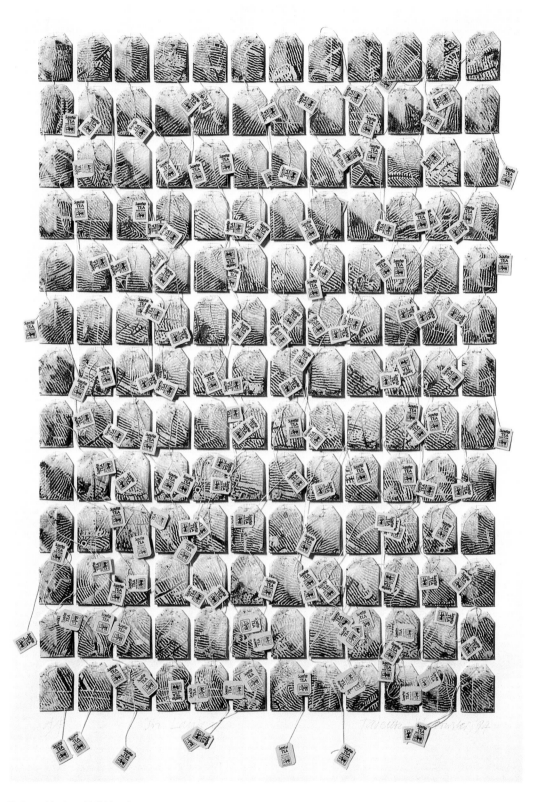

Tadeusz Nuckowski **Sri Lanka**
1994, Linocut on Ceylon Tea Bags, 100 x 70 cm. Collection of the artist. Photograph: T. Nuckowski

Tadeusz Nuckowski **Putative Intention**
1995, Linocut, 73 x 53 cm. Collection of the artist. Photograph: T. Nuckowski

Tadeusz Nuckowski **Bottle in the Grass**
1996, Linocut on aluminium foil on bottle of Hungarian semi-dry white wine. Collection of the artist
Photograph: T. Nuckowski

Ryszard Otreba

Ryszard Otreba was born in Suszec in 1932 and studied art and design at the Academy of Fine Arts in Krakow from 1953–59, graduating as Master of Fine Arts. Since 1960 he has taught at the Academy and is currently Professor of Visual Art and Design in the Faculty of Industrial Design. He has held guest professorships in Sydney, Helsinki and Connecticut, has curated exhibitions in many countries and has served on the juries of many important international exhibitions as well as on the committees of numerous international institutions. In addition, his personal work in printmaking and drawing has been widely exhibited, is included in many important collections throughout the world and has led to him receiving over seventy awards. He has worked extensively in the fields of design and visual communications, undertaking numerous research and practical projects. This broad area of activity in an international context marks Otreba as an exceptional contributor to the Polish art scene.

While his work in printmaking includes examples using silkscreen and linocut, he is held in high regard for his pioneering development of the medium of plastercut. The brittle surface of gypsum plaster provides the artist with a challenging matrix but Otreba's mastery of the technique of cutting into the surface and then producing prints on Japanese rice paper, usually restricting himself to a range of black inks with the occasional use of colour, has resulted in an impressive series of works. The process is necessarily a slow one which demands a high level of intellectual control and concentration as well as technical excellence, throughout which he must hold true to the basic conception from which he starts. While it may appear that Otreba's work is clinically abstract, and indeed it is non-figurative in that his images consist of geometrical areas combined with successive areas of parallel lines, it is derived from an emotional response to personal situations. This gives his work an added resonance which accounts for the intensity of feeling that comes from prints that might otherwise be seen as coldly considered constructions of black on white. Writing to the compiler of the London Tate Gallery's *Illustrated Catalogue of Acquisitions 1984–86* he stressed the personal and private nature of his series 'Letters to my Wife', adding: 'They are made for one person only — almost like writing a letter to somebody who is a very close friend, a lover — just my wife'.

Thus, the complexity and perfection of Otreba's work come from the combination of a deeply personal basis, a time-consuming technical process and an acute knowledge of the scientific and psychological complexities of visual communication by means of signs and images.

On a purely visual level, the prints are finely considered compositions in which light and dark areas are combined to give static images that nonetheless have a strong sense of spatial complexity which is not revealed by a cursory glance but requires contemplation. In this sense they achieve the quality of icons, not with a specific focus such as is found in traditional religious iconographic paintings but with an emotional focus that has a profound spiritual element, that of a personal expression of the 'sacrum' within human experience, one freed from the restrictions of sentiment. While they may have their origin in a very personal sense of meaning to the artist it is, however, not necessary to have knowledge of this in order to be able to appreciate them as they are capable of invoking a personal response in the viewer which depends on each individual person's consideration of their own attitude to emotional and physical experience.

Abstraction in art contains the risk of the artist retreating into the use of a self-referential vocabulary of form and colour justified by the application of mathematical rules and formulae which deny any form of emotional basis. This risk has led, understandably in the case of artists living through a time of tumultuous social and political change such as has affected Poland in recent years, to many of them turning back to figuration as the means for expression. On the other hand, a significant number of Polish artists have continued to use non-figurative means of expression and this has resulted in a distinct polarisation in that country's art scene. What is also significant is that their approach to abstraction is frequently based on a strong sense of human spirituality, and the work of Ryszard Otreba is a prime example of this, providing the opportunity for a deeper consideration of the role of artistic expression within the framework of human experience.

Ryszard Otreba **Sign Limitation I**
1990, Silkscreen and linocut, 75 x 54 cm. Collection of the artist. Photograph: Janusz Kozina

Ryszard Otreba **Imaginary Disappearance of an Object**
1990, Plasterprint, 80 x 59 cm. Collection of the artist

Ryszard Otreba **Sign Discrimination VI**
1992, Plasterprint, 79 x 58 cm. Collection of the artist

Henryk **Ozog**

Henryk Ozog was born in Wysoka in 1956 and studied printmaking at the Academy of Fine Arts in Krakow from 1976–81, graduating from the studios of Professors Mieczyslaw Wejman and Witold Skulicz. He lives in Krakow, teaches at the Academy and has had individual exhibitions in Poland, France, Australia and Switzerland, as well as participating in group exhibitions in many parts of the world.

At the beginning of his career Ozog made small prints that set the direction he was to follow but, in the mid-1980s, a time of growing confidence in the country after the hardships of the early part of the decade, he began to produce a series of large black and white drypoints, finding that this technique of graving directly into a metal plate without the need for the complexities of etching and aquatint suited his desire to obtain a 'drawn' image with the same sense of freedom that comes with the use of a pencil. Drypoint, particularly at a large size, is a demanding skill in which the manipulation of the burin can achieve a wide variation in the type of line produced. Ozog used this characteristic to the full, producing areas of softness and subtly varied tone as well as the hard line of engraving, earning the admiration of his contemporaries as well as the critics. Visual flair has since become a keynote of this artist's work. In the work that followed he introduced colour through the technique of aquatint and it is this combination that he employs more than any other in his current work, allowing him a flexibility that approaches that of painting while still retaining the possibility of producing his works in editions.

There is a sense of playfulness in his use of printmaking techniques which extends as much to the manner in which he uses imagery as it does to his use of technique. At first glance there are resemblances to the work of David Hockney and Francis Bacon, and superficially this remains so. However, Ozog's sensibilities derive from a situation very different from the post-war angst of Bacon and the camp iconography of Hockney. He does, however, share in part Bacon's approach to the way in which the faces and figures in his work are treated, their features scrubbed out, rendered indistinctive, and also Hockney's use of disparate images within a single print. In a way this could be seen as a disadvantage in that the use of such images as swimming pools, bathrooms and modern interiors, with their angular plants and geometric furniture, has in many people's view become a Hockney trademark. Ozog, however, works in such a way that these apparent derivations can be discounted, producing works that have a greater sense of postmodernism in that they quote from or refer to a disparate range of sources. His prints are emphatically not narrative, the stories to be told lie concealed behind the scattered images and do not have a single interpretation.

It would be pointless to ascribe to these works the description of landscape, interior, still life or portrait as they do not have any sense of the unifying structure that such descriptions require. Instead they operate within their own terms of reference, constructing a vision of a world in which everything can happen all at once, independent of a defined framework. They do not disallow the viewer to decide on a particular meaning but do not require it either: they provide a set of colours, shapes and forms that may or may not coalesce into something concrete, but if they do not then there is always the sense of vitality and illusion that shifts with each viewing.

Defying logic, these works need to be considered as describing the events, fantasies and visionary dreams experienced by a young artist for whom the exploration of technique and the making of art are in themselves vital experiences. In a way they may be seen as interim works, for there is an energy within them that has not reached a point of stasis. Henryk Ozog lives in a country in which much that surrounds him is undergoing rapid evolution and is developing into a society very different from that which existed at the time of his graduation. While some artists choose to have a quieter viewpoint from which to observe these changes, he instead puts himself on the energetic edge where there is a different sense of risk, and where a necessary sense of confusion has an important part to play.

Henryk Ozog **Dilemma**
1993, Intaglio, 70 x 100 cm. Collection of the artist

Henryk Ozog **A Dog**
1991, Intaglio, 65 x 100 cm. Collection of the artist

Henryk Ozog **A Park**
1994, Intaglio, 70 x 100 cm. Collection of the artist

Jan **Pamula**

Until relatively recently computer technology had not had a great impact on Polish society and the lack of availability of this as a tool for artists meant that very little work in this field was done. The rapid developments in the country have brought sophisticated technology within the reach of many and with this has come an increase in the number of artists exploring its use, either in its own right or as an adjunct to work in other mediums. Jan Pamula is in the forefront of those graphic artists for whom the computer has become an important tool. He was born in Spytkowice in 1944 and studied at the Krakow Academy of Fine Arts from 1961–68, spending 1967 at the École Nationale Supèrieur des Beaux Arts in Paris, and graduated as Master of Fine Arts from the departments of Painting and Graphic Arts in 1968. He lives in Krakow and since 1975 has taught at the Academy, where he is currently Professor in the Department of Industrial Design. He was the recipient of scholarships from the French Government in 1980, the Kosciuszko Foundation (New York) in 1982 and was Fulbright Scholar at the NYIT in 1993. In 1992 he was a visiting professor at the University of Connecticut. He has shown his work widely in individual and group exhibitions in many parts of the world and it is also in many international public and private collections.

Pamula initially produced paintings and prints in a figurative style, but soon embarked on the program of essentially abstract works that has occupied him ever since. From 1972–92 he worked on a major series of paintings, colour lithographs and etchings under the title 'Systems'. The basic visual form is that of a rectangle surmounted by a semicircle, within which a rigidly defined set of rectangles and radiused forms are contained. While the forms are defined by geometry the colours used are determined according to their role as what the artist terms 'abstract psycho-physical entities', following a strict system of hues and intensities. While the results of his work in this series, recently extended to include computer-generated works, are essentially abstract, they nonetheless bear with them references to the physical world, recalling doorways, gates, windows, painted altar-pieces and Jewish tombstones. The artist writes of them that, 'As abstract compositions they are the expression of a pure spirituality, as symbolic signs they are "mystical gates" pointing to another reality'.

The systems approach is crucial to Pamula as is its expression, until recently, through conventional fine art mediums. The combination gives his work a positive structure based on mathematics and, at the same time, shows the evidence of adherence to pure artistic methods. From 1980–95 he worked on a long series of paintings based on computer drawings. The program used gave him a succession of purely abstract drawings composed of multiple rectangles of the same proportions of which no two have precisely the same dimensions. He took these drawings and enlarged them as paintings on canvas in which the colours follow strictly controlled rules. Some of these large paintings are dedicated to other artists according to the range of hues used. The emotional resonance of works from this series is considerable.

In 1992 Pamula extended his use of computer technology to produce a cycle of prints under the title 'Leonardo'. He scanned reproductions of paintings by Leonardo da Vinci into a computer and then manipulated the images using a commercial photo-processing system. The results show familiar excerpts subverted through the technology to give repetitions, reversals, changes of scale and colour, and compressions, arranged together with other elements such as circles and ellipses according to predetermined rules, then realised as prints on a high-quality colour printer. One cannot but think that Leonardo would have approved and would, had the technology been available to him, have done much the same himself.

In his recent work Pamula has returned to the use of abstract imagery, using a computer program to give variations on a theme. Ellipses composed of swirls of colour or rectangles are combined with vertical bands of colour to create the illusion of depth. The colours are intense yet controlled, the resulting images abstract and profound. There are those who doubt that computer technology, however sophisticated it may be, can ever create art that can stand comparison with that produced by traditional means. The work of Jan Pamula, exploring as it does what is still a new frontier for art, points to the opposite conclusion.

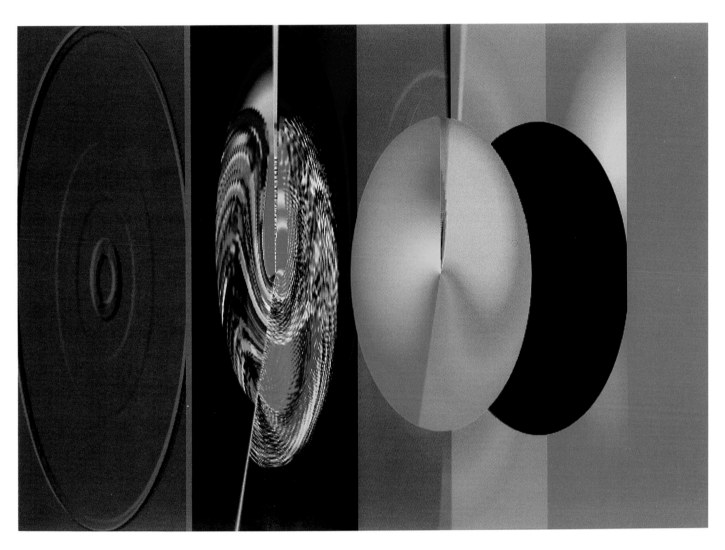

Jan Pamula **Image 9**
1994, Computer print, 32 x 40.5 cm. Collection of the artist

Jan Pamula **System 7b**
1992, Computer print, 42 x 30 cm. Collection of the artist

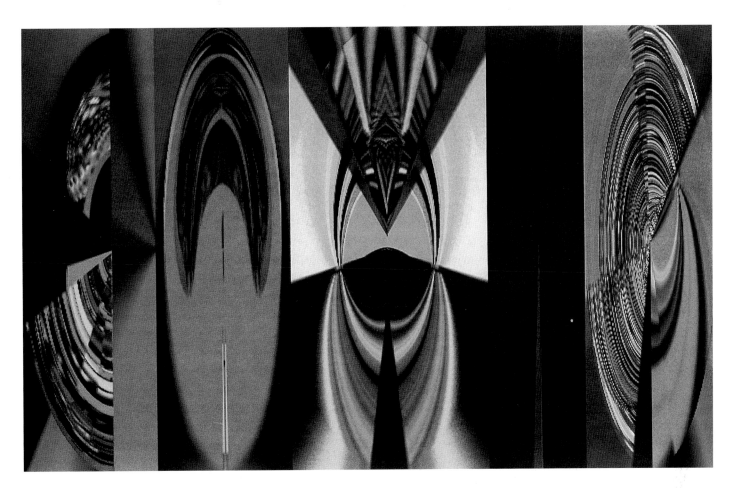

Jan Pamula **NY 7b**
1994, Computer print, 32 x 40.5 cm. Collection of the artist

Marcin **Pawlowski**

Drawing, strictly defined in the *Concise Oxford Dictionary*, is the 'art of representing by line, delineation without colour or with single colour'. This narrow definition has been breached in many recent exhibitions of 'drawing' and in the writings of many artists who seek to extend it to include 'marks made on paper'. If this extension of the definition is right then the work of Marcin Pawlowski falls into the category of drawing. It has been a characteristic of avant-garde artists in Poland, as elsewhere throughout the 20th century, to refuse narrow limitations and to push forward the boundaries of what art can include. As they have done so the process of time has allowed the assimilation of the new into the accepted canons of art: the new does not remain so for long.

Marcin Pawlowski was born in Krakow in 1954 and studied there at the Academy of Fine Art from 1975–80, graduating from the Department of Graphic Arts. He currently works at the Higher Pedagogical College in Krakow. Since his graduation he has practised drawing, photography and the creation of 'actions in natural space', participating in many important group exhibitions in Poland as well as having individual exhibitions of his work in Poland and Germany. He has written of the objective circumstances of his work in which, having determined the rules which the construction process he uses must follow, the element of indeterminacy plays an important part. For him the intervention of the absolute qualities of geometry, arithmetic and mechanics are, through their rigour and intransigence, the 'philosophy, message and technique of art, all at the same time'. This firm stance has the effect of introducing the element of 'otherness' into his work, allowing him to detach himself from the notion that he, as the artist, is the only one responsible for it. There is a precedent for this approach in the work of a number of Polish artists in the past twenty-five years and while many more used to looking at drawing made by more conventional means may find such work difficult or easily dismissed, it is nonetheless an important ingredient of the present Polish art scene.

Working in series is, given the nature of his approach, essential for Pawlowski, as a single outcome from an intellectually constructed process would be insufficient to allow it to reach its conclusion: as befits this approach the series are numbered. 'Rysunek VI' ('Drawings VI') from 1992 used the technique of painting bands of colour in gouache on paper, some with ragged edges, others with straight edges, then cutting these into narrow strips of even width. The strips of colour thus produced were a solid colour, white paper with traces of colour or unpainted. They were then arranged according to a set of rules devised by the artist so that they formed squares of fixed dimensions with the ends of the strips numbered and taped into position. The full set of drawings thus produced comprised the finished work, in which the elementary forms of the plus and minus signs were made apparent.

'Rysunek VII' ('Drawing VII'), two of which are illustrated here, took the idea further, using a wider range of colours and tones to construct a total of forty-eight square elements which were arranged, for their exhibition at the Parochialkirche in Berlin in 1995, in grids according to the application of a chance method. The images that resulted create a visual language of signs in which that of each element combines with others in each set to give a shifting sense of abstract meaning. In *8 Rysunkow (8 Drawings)*, 1994 (also illustrated), Pawlowski adopted a different approach. Each work was made in pencil and gouache according to an essentially simple formula whereby squares of paper, painted in gouache so that the brush marks remained, were marked along their edges with pairs of points determined according to a set of rules involving chance. Each pair of marks (there are three on each edge) is joined to those on the next edge by curved lines of regular width and painted so that the tones change at each meeting of edges and a continuous loop, or set of loops, is created. The fascination of this work comes from attempting to decode the process that has created it. Pawlowski's work is very much that of an explorer who has set himself a rigid agenda and offers an insight into one avant-garde approach to contemporary drawing in Poland.

Marcin Pawlowski From the series **Rysunek VII (Drawing VII)**
1994, Two elements from the series, Gouache, 60 x 63 cm. Collection of the artist

Marcin Pawlowski From the series **8 Rysunkow (8 Drawings)**
1994, Pencil, gouache, 60 x 60 cm. Collection of the artist

Leszek Rozga **Monument**
1996, Dryprint and watercolour. Collection of the artist

Leszek Rozga **Double**
1995, Dryprint and ink. Collection of the artist

Leszek Rozga **Three on the Desert**
1996, Etching. Collection of the artist

Krzysztof **Roziewicz**

Krzysztof Roziewicz was born in Zydardow in 1955. He studied at the Warsaw Academy of Fine Arts from 1986–91, graduating from the graphics studio of the late Professor Roman Artymowski, who was an important part of Poland's artistic life in the middle part of this century as well as being a highly regarded teacher. Roziewicz also studied drawing under the guidance of Professor Julian Raczko. He lives in Warsaw, has exhibited widely in Poland and elsewhere in Europe and the United States and was the recipient of a scholarship from the Ministry of Culture.

The work of this artist, mostly in mezzotint, which is a technically demanding technique, has an instantly recognisable mysterious presence. While it is concerned with the traditional theme of landscape it is by no means topographical: it refers not to any specific location but rather to a place in the imagination that is still somehow familiar. These landscapes are silent places, mythic without being illustrative, belonging more to the Romantic tradition than any other, reminiscent in some way of the work of Casper David Friedrich, yet not derivative. The places Roziewicz depicts are not fixed in any particular time; they have instead a quality of the eternal, of having always been there. Their attraction lies in their ability to engender remembrance and a sense of identification with the particular characteristics of each print. Professor Raczko, writing of the artist's work, describes it as creating 'a space which seems to have no contact with reality. Light and shapes are quite different from those created by nature. It is not an imitation of any landscape. His compositions do not reflect common ideas of the general knowledge of the world but speak of self-evident truths about the feelings of a human being who is surrounded by the continuously passing reality of the world'. Raczko also draws a parallel between the work of Roziewicz and music in that he sees in it a relationship between the graphic structures and those, such as harmony, rhythm and composition, in music.

The quality of light within these prints is such that the source of light is not always easy to discern — it appears to be without direction, diffused by the murky atmosphere, and even the time of day is uncertain. The skies, if skies they are, are veiled in cloud and the distance is lost in a diffused mist. Forms resembling trees appear like blunted spears, leafless and mostly without branches, and the surface from which they emerge is creased and folded into immense valleys. The bleakness of the world depicted is perhaps that which has resulted from a nuclear holocaust or some pervasive pollution: human presence is neither depicted nor implied and the absence of anything resembling life is palpable. Later prints in the series concentrate on what appears to be a closer view, with rock-like forms appearing from a smooth surface, or with curved shapes like thorns covering a sloping plane. Seen as a series these prints tell of a place in the imagination of Roziewicz which is obviously real to him. It is interesting to consider how this relates to the real environment in which he lives, for, while some parts of Poland such as Upper Silesia are industrialised and among the most heavily polluted places on earth, other areas are still wide open plains, little changed by the tides of history that have swept across them, and remnants of the primeval European forest still exist near the border with Belarus.

Krzysztof Roziewicz is still at the beginning of his career but has clearly embarked already on a unique and ambitious program of work. The country in which he lives is developing rapidly into a modern European economy, a process that will bring far-reaching changes to every aspect of the culture and life of the people. What these changes might be is difficult to see but it is certain that many aspects of the Poland in which he grew up will no longer be the same. This artist's vision is based on a serious view not only of the techniques he pursues and the images that result but also of the relevance of his art to the times in which he lives. It has added interest in that it does not fit comfortably into the history of 20th-century Polish printmaking, having a distinct relationship to developments which are more international. In itself this does not present a problem in that art can be, to varying measures, independent of national trends and identities. The resonances of the work he has produced until now are far reaching.

Krzysztof Roziewicz **Landscape III**
1991, Mezzotint, 64.5 x 49.5 cm. Collection of the artist

Krzysztof Roziewicz **Landscape II**
1991, Mezzotint, 64.5 x 49 cm. Collection of the artist

Tadeusz Michal Siara From the series **W Wiezy Babel, R (In the Tower of Babel, R)**
1989, Etching, 12 x 10 cm. Collection of the artist

Wieslaw Skibinski

Wieslaw Skibinski was born in Limanowa in 1961 and studied in the Graphic Art Department of the Krakow Academy of Fine Arts from 1982–87, graduating from the studios of Professors Jerzy Kucia and Stanislaw Wejman. He lives in Tychy and practises printmaking, drawing, animated film and photography. He is a member of the TE7EM group. His work has been shown in individual and group exhibitions in Poland and other countries including Japan, and he won prizes for his animated film *Cztery pory roku (Four Seasons of the Year)* in Zamosc in 1988 and Bielsko-Biala in 1989.

There is a playfulness in Skibinski's work which belies the seriousness of his approach. He works mostly in etching and linocut, sometimes combining the two techniques in one print, an infrequent practice in printmaking but one which gives his work a distinct character. He also uses relief together with etching. The simplicity of this artist's prints are deceptive: although the resulting forms may appear basic, even bordering on the naive, they are in fact the outcome of a long process of refinement and creative experimentation, during which he eliminates all unnecessary elements until he is left with what for him is the bare minimum that his concept requires. His training at the Academy gave him an appreciation of the traditional techniques of printmaking and the discipline that they impose on the artist, but he, like others of his generation in Krakow, has chosen to depart from the strictures of those traditions. In the case of Skibinski, the making of a print is an individual activity for, although the possibilities of producing an edition exist within the processes he uses, his method of working is closer to the unique nature of painting. This attitude runs counter to the idea of the atelier print in which the production of a numbered edition of prints of equal quality is a guiding imperative. Writing of the work of Skibinski and others (including Bogdan Achimescu) Jan Fejkiel, who runs a successful graphics gallery in Krakow, has commented: 'It is a paradox that the shallow nature of our art market works to their advantage, as their principles are not put in jeopardy by big orders. Or, perhaps, one should perceive these creative efforts as radical conclusions drawn from the characteristics of Polish graphic art'.[1]

The images produced by Skibinski are visually uncluttered, consisting of simple shapes, sometimes repeated in pairs to give something approaching the effect of a mirror. These images tend towards being interpretations of elements in the world around him or from his imagination and memory. Imperfection and deformation appeal to the artist, his forms being derived from his visual experience and then subjected to analysis and reduction until they become abstractions, in which colour plays an important part. There is nothing in the background of the forms presented — they are placed on the whiteness of the paper, often leaving a wide area in which the forms float. Deprived of spatial and temporal references the forms appear to exist in reference only to themselves, enabling them to be considered in isolation. This process allows the artist to push the potential of his medium to the limit and in so doing to re-invent many of the concepts of printmaking, producing results that subvert the initial sense of naivety with images of refreshing sophistication.

Many of Skibinski's prints take angels and devils as their subject matter, shown not as ethereal or evil forms but with an elemental simplicity that reduces them to much the same level, although with different connotations. There is levity in these images, far removed from the traditional ways in which they have been depicted in religious art over the centuries, but perhaps with more relevance to increasingly secular times. The three images shown here cover some of the concerns of Wieslaw Skibinski. *Two Smokes*, 1994, resembles houses drawn by a child, the doorways and windows askew and architecturally unlikely. The forms are balanced in both shape and colour, the windows forming a curve that is balanced by the doorways and chimneys, from which come impressed puffs of smoke (which are so subtle that they unfortunately do not reproduce well). *Gudzia*, 1994, is a strange boar-like creature, reduced to a massive bulk decorated in viridian green with a pronounced snout, that looks as if it has wandered out of a fairy story, while *Barbakan*, 1992, is a fanciful interpretation of the defensive tower, a remnant, in the style of medieval Turkish architecture, of the ancient Krakow defensive walls. In Skibinski's version the conical pinnacles curl skywards like smoke.

1. Catalogue for 'Grafika Alternatywna', Jan Fejkiel Gallery, Krakow, 1995.

Wieslaw Skibinski **Gudzia**
1994, Etching and relief, 37 x 56 cm. Collection of the artist. Photograph: Pawel Chawinski

Wieslaw Skibinski **Two Smokes**
1994, Etching, 50 x 64 cm. Collection of the artist. Photograph: Pawel Chawinski

Wieslaw Skibinski **Barbakan**
1992, Etching, 25.3 x 34.7 cm. Collection of the artist. Photograph: Pawel Chawinski

Krzysztof **Skorczewski**

Krzysztof Skorczewski was born in Krakow, where he still lives, in 1947 and studied there at the Academy of Fine Arts, graduating in 1971. He studied also with Professor Nils Stenqvist at the Royal School of Art in Stockholm in 1976 where he was introduced to the traditional and highly refined technique of copper engraving — the medium in which most of his considerable output of work has been produced. In recent years he has produced also cycles of drawings in pastel, a medium that differs greatly from engraving. His work has been shown in over one hundred individual and group exhibitions in Poland and internationally and is considered to be among the most accomplished work in copper engraving currently being produced.

As mentioned previously in this book, the technique of copper engraving is one of the most challenging available to the artist. In one sense it is a daunting technique upon which to embark in that it demands not only manual dexterity but also a rigourous intellectual process, with the necessity of maintaining a high level of concentration over an extended period of time. In addition, it is a medium in which the historical antecedents are so highly regarded that many artists do not seek to emulate the achievements of such predecessors as Durer, Mantegna and Pollaiuolo. That Skorczewski has done so with such a high degree of success marks him justifiably as a contemporary master of the technique, a technique that requires a finely tuned control of the burin when cutting lines into the polished copper sheet in the preparation of the plate as well as a sophisticated level of awareness of the possibilities inherent in the choice and use of inks during the printing process itself. Skorczewski engages himself in both parts of the process rather than, as some artists do, leaving the printing of the edition to skilled craftsmen.

The mastery of a technique is, however, not enough to ensure excellent work: there is also the need to consider the manner in which imagery is used and presented in the final work. In this sense also this artist has achieved extraordinary results. Due to the complexities of the technique many copper engravings are, compared with works in linocut, lithography or etching, small in scale, but some of Skorczewski's prints are as large as 35 cm x 50 cm, in itself a major achievement. The scale can be deceptive, however, as he has developed a lexicon of images that belies the relatively small scale of the prints — one can with justification describe them as being of epic proportion and grandeur. An early print, *Narodziny Wenus (The Birth of Venus)*, 1977–78, offers a radically different vision of the mythological event from that of Botticelli. For Skorczewski, the figure of Venus is not that of a nubile maiden decorously emerging from gentle waves onto an idyllic beach. His Venus emerges alone, half reptile, half mature woman, from a stormy wave in a barren landscape beneath a cloud-swept sky, her back arched with tension in her evolution from the ocean world to that of the air. The world into which she comes is further described in the prints that follow.

There are echoes of Breughel and Piranesi in many of this artist's prints but they are acknowledgments rather than quotations. There are towers and other vast edifices, partly constructed or partly crumbling, propped up by the wooden scaffolding that is still sometimes seen in contemporary Poland, reaching towards heavy skies. These structures are clearly the work of humans, yet human figures are absent or only hinted at in tiny forms within the structures. The overriding impression is of emptiness and silence, of futility and despair, as these most ambitious structures fall prey to the processes of time. The destruction is implied or, as in *Potop (Flood)*, 1985, explicit. In this print a torrent pours from the sky to inundate a cyclopean structure, the inevitable fate of humanity's vaunting ambition. In some of the prints from 1995, such as *Drzewo (Tree)* or *Ogrod (Garden)*, the atmosphere is calmer, but the skills of the artist remain as acute as ever. The symbolism shifts, in response perhaps to the changing times in which Krzysztof Skorczewski lives, but the questions regarding humanity's place in the scheme of things remain. The apocalyptic vision of this artist, expressed with a rare skill, is a testament to the integrity of Poland's artists at the end of the 20th century. It will be instructive to see how his work develops into the new millennium.

Krzysztof Skorczewski **Oko Wszechswiata (The Eye of the Universe)**
1991, Copper engraving, 23 x 24 cm. Collection of the artist

Krzysztof Skorczewski **Potop (Flood)**
1985, Copper engraving, 27 x 39 cm. Collection of the artist

Krzysztof Skorczewski **Klatka (Cage)**
1988, Copper engraving, 9.9 x 9.2 cm. Collection of the artist

Jacek Sroka

Jacek Sroka was born in 1957 in Krakow where he studied painting and graphic art at the Academy of Fine Arts, graduating in 1981 from the studios of Professors Mieczyslaw Wejman and Witold Skulicz. He worked as an assistant in the Graphic Art Department from 1981–89, since which time he has devoted himself to his work in painting, drawing and printmaking, exhibiting widely throughout the world and receiving numerous important international awards.

Sroka's work has been linked to that of the German Expressionists such as Grosz and Beckmann and to artists such as Clemente and Paladino of the Italian *transavanguardia* as well as to the *Neue Wilde* tendency that emerged in Europe in the 1980s. While such links are not without substance, as the artist would be the first to admit, there are deeper undercurrents in his work that mark it as being specifically Polish. In particular, it is not incorrect to look back to the wistful and mysterious paintings of Witold Wojtkiewicz, the symbolist painter active at the beginning of the century, or to the powerfully imaginative work of Witkiewicz ('Witkacy'), active in the early decades of the century, to see some of the same approaches that Sroka uses but in no sense replicates. In the work of those two artists there is combined the imaginative power of the visionary and the deep-seated concern of the Poles for the nature of their society and the history of their country. Sroka's work will in due course come to be seen as an important historical record as it provides a particularly sharp insight into the manner in which an artist has responded to and commented on the social and political turmoil of the past fifteen years and all the massive changes that have come about as a result.

However, this artist's work is not didactic; it does not illustrate political events but rather comments on them elliptically, often with a wry sense of humour and elements of the bizarre. He is an acutely aware observer of human foibles and the many small ridiculous positions that people find themselves in. At the same time he is able to place events and characters outside specific locations in time and space so that they become symbols or metaphors for modern society. Sroka's output in all the mediums that he pursues is considerable and his fertile imagination continues to develop, sometimes unpredictably. His work in printmaking and drawing has developed considerably in recent years, maturing from the chaotic images he produced (quite appropriately) in the 1980s to others which have a greater sense of order, without having yet achieved calm. The passion with which he reveals the objects of his love and hatred — his love of the good that remains in the world and his hatred of all overpowering authority, be it military, political or ecclesiastical, as well as his abiding fear of dogs — remains unsullied. His hatred of power is expressed not so much through polemic, but through a calculated attack using irony, sarcasm and black humour to point to the absurdities of those whose sole purpose in life seems to be the exercise of power over others.

For all these characteristics Sroka remains true to the development of his art according to the tried and trusted techniques that he uses. Just as his painting is extremely well made, using colour with assurance and considerable judgment, his printmaking is the development of the excellence of his predecessors in Poland. Mieczyslaw Wejman remains a highly regarded artist as well as a respected teacher and Sroka learnt much from him, as he did from Stanislaw Wejman, his Professor's son, with whom he collaborated for a number of years in the 1980s, developing a type of etching with aquatint that was technically highly refined and used colour in a new and expressive manner.

The work upon which Sroka is currently engaged bears witness to strong and fertile roots, as the examples of his work illustrated here show. There is a mysterious malevolence in *Eight*, 1992, which hints at some hidden power, a warning perhaps of the 'worm in the bud', of the darkness that lies beyond the doors of seats of power. *House of Evil*, 1995, is about no particular country but concerns rather the potential for domination through fear that lies at the heart of all despotic governments, while *Man Tuning in TV Set (Berlin 37)*, 1990, is an apt judgment on the power of global communications. Jacek Sroka remains a distinctively Polish artist, but one whose work has international relevance and importance.

Jacek Sroka **Eight**
1992, Etching and aquatint, 46.5 x 50 cm. Collection of the artist

Jacek Sroka **House of Evil**
1995, Etching and aquatint, 44.5 x 61 cm. Collection of the artist

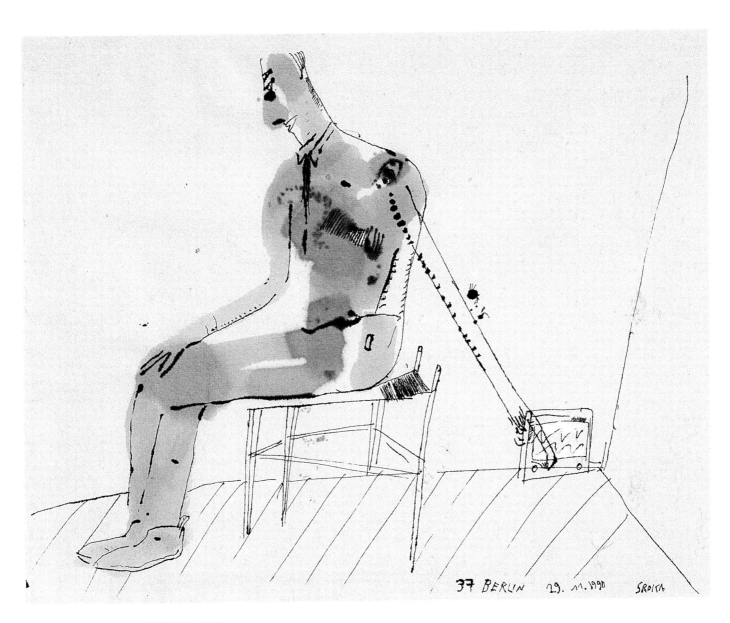

Jacek Sroka **Man Tuning in TV Set (Berlin 37)**
1990, Drawing, ink and wash on paper, 31 x 44 cm. Collection of the artist

Marcin **Surzycki**

One of the younger generation of Polish artists working in printmaking, Marcin Surzycki has already established a name for the originality and quality of his work through his participation in a considerable number of international and Polish group exhibitions. He was born in Poznan in 1963 and studied in Krakow, where he now lives, first at the High School of Arts and then in the Graphics Department of the Academy of Fine Arts (during which time he was awarded a scholarship from the Ministry of Culture), graduating from the studio of Professor Andrzej Pietsch in 1989. His career therefore began at a time when his country's economic position was starting to improve and a greater sense of confidence was evident in Poland, unlike the situation that faced those artists who graduated in the difficult times of the period of Martial Law some ten years earlier or in the difficult years of transition that followed, whose attitudes and the work they produced were affected by these events.

In common with many other young artists, not only those in Poland, Surzycki prefers to develop his own techniques rather than to follow slavishly the tried and trusted techniques of the past. His education at the Academy provided him with the necessary understanding and experience of traditional techniques but also gave him a broadly based understanding of what art can achieve if the limits are not accepted as being fixed. There is an aspect of painting in his approach to printmaking: the scale of much of his work, with dimensions around 100 cm, takes it closer to painting, as does his use of colour and form. There is something of the brash rawness of Pop Art in his work, the taking of simple elements and then reducing them towards a minimum, using bright colours with hard edges. However, while such a simplistic analysis is not without some basis, it does not sum up this artist's work satisfactorily, and does not take into account the very different circumstances that exist in contemporary Poland compared with those in Western Europe and North America in the late 1960s.

Surzycki's technique in the making of the matrix involves building it up with sand and lacquer to create a very resistant and textured surface, which gives his works something of the character of relief prints when they are made on heavy paper. Combined with a careful choice of colour materials, the surface richness that results gives his prints a unique and recognisable identity, allowing his images to achieve a real sense of strength and confidence. The themes of this artist's work fall into a number of series. In a set of head and shoulder portraits he depicts such characters as *Number One*, a tennis player wearing a baseball cap that casts a shadow over his face, from within which eyes reduced to blue lights peer (the background is a red tennis court). In *Favourite* a man wears what appears to be a legal gown and powdered wig, his face is orange, his eyes blank, his mouth firmly closed. *Black Widow* is a woman in black, her mouth a malevolent red scar. In all three the highly textured and coloured surface produced by the artist's technique add to the haunting effect. *Red Man* and *Black Man* are head and shoulder portraits of men with wide shoulders and tiny heads, their elegant hands hold cups and saucers; they are perhaps minor civic functionaries, symbolised as is appropriate.

Two prints, *Afternoon* and *Evening*, demonstrate a different approach. In each a single piece of period furniture is shown against a blank background, the curvilinear form and the use of strong colour giving it an almost animal personality. This process of reduction is shown also in three prints from 1994, *Stairs I, Stairs II* and *Arena*. In these the viewer is presented with a very large simple form, each in tones of a single colour, and an abstraction of an architectural element. It is not clear from which position in space and time they come, they refer only to themselves. In addition, the forms are cut out from the paper on which they are printed so that they are even isolated from the conventional notion of print. In 1996 the artist returned to the theme of portrait in a series of images of heads produced using a stencil technique that minimalises further the conventional notion of what a portrait should be. The production of unique prints according to a highly individual agenda gives Marcin Surzycki's work a valuable position within current Polish printmaking.

Marcin Surzycki **Stairs I**
1994, Own technique, intaglio, 140 x 76 cm. Collection of the artist

Marcin Surzycki **Arena**
1994, Own technique, intaglio, 100 x 150 cm. Collection of the artist

Marcin Surzycki **Fryderyk**
1996, Stencil, 50 x 54 cm. Collection of the artist

Jacek Szewczyk

Jacek Szewczyk was born in Wroclaw where he trained at the Academy of Fine Art and Design, graduating with honours in 1982 from the studios of Professors H. Pawlikowska and J. J. Aleksiun. He has taught graphic art at the Academy since his graduation as well as showing his own work in printmaking and drawing at many exhibitions throughout the world, winning a number of prizes including the Gold Medal and First Prize at the 3rd International Biennale of Engraving in Orense in 1994.

Wroclaw, in particular Zeglarska Street where he lives, provides the location from which his works are derived. This is not to say that his work is in any way topological, for it is not, neither for that matter is it logical in the normal sense of the word, containing its own crazy sense of order in the chaotic distribution of the images which cluster in each piece of work. The underlying humour that pervades this artist's work in etching and drawing is infectious, with a multitude of small images filling each sheet of paper. Given that Szewczyk works on a large scale — his etchings are often 100 cm x 70 cm, his drawings frequently larger — the temptation to seek some form of narrative in his work is irresistible, but in vain. The references within his work are many, some private reflections on his immediate surroundings, others derived from literature (he is fascinated by the works of Mikhail Bulgakov, Kafka and Dostoyevsky, as well as by the productions of Kantor and Polanski) or from his imagination. The relationships between the various parts of each work are not always clear, nor are they intended to be. Instead, Szewczyk presents a world that operates entirely according to its own rules, echoing the urban madness of daily life in which haste is paramount, relationships between the people who crowd together there are tenuous at best, aggressive at worst, and the clutter of signs, objects and waste is all pervasive. Significantly, the artist chooses techniques that require a great deal of time, concentration and painstaking effort.

The part of Wroclaw in which the artist lives is unremarkable but it provides a potent source of inspiration. He says of it: 'I set a high value on the simplicity of associations and authenticity: and so, speaking of Zeglarska Street, it is the simplest thing that comes to mind. I draw my immediate world — in this case it is a street. The situation that I want to talk about is laid near my house, under my eyes. And that is important to me'.[1] It is unlikely that other residents of Zeglarska Street would recognise immediately their street in Szewczyk's drawings because his interpretation of it is enveloped in fantasy and humour. However, the essential character of any ordinary street is left intact, depicting the ordinariness in which the unusual conjunctions of things or events are taken as being perfectly normal. In this sense there is something of the surrealist in Szewczyk.

Wheeled vehicles (bicycles, carts, curious contraptions) appear frequently in his work, there are strange wooden railways that defy the laws of perspective, buildings made of what appears to be metal or wooden parts roughly fitted together to form egg-like structures, objects hang in the air or fly through it, figures make their way through their unremarkable lives in remarkable places or stand about, all in what appears to them to be perfectly ordinary situations. In producing these works Szewczyk ignores the normal conventions of perspective and composition. His is not a version of classical academic art, it does not fit easily within the canons of figuration — it is light, irreverent, decidedly humorous and yet serious at the same time. It does not, moreover, make sociological or political comments, unless the viewer wishes to put them there.

The works chosen for illustration here show some of the aspects of Jacek Szewczyk's current work. *Gorale (The Mountaineers)*, 1993, is a story of the people of the southern mountains. They wear traditional costumes, the visitors wear skiing outfits, the bicycles are there and, of course, ladders reach into the sky. *Specially for the Very Narrow-Gauge Railway*, 1993, is a snapshot of everyday life in which the crazy illogicality with which the elements are juxtaposed seems perfectly acceptable, while *The Breslauers*, 1994 (Breslau is the old German name for Wroclaw), simply go about their everyday business, concerned only for the moment. The world depicted here is full of incident, detail and, above all, great good humour.

1. Quoted by Jakub Kostowski in 'What's going on in Zeglarska Street', *Format* 1–2, 1995.

Jacek Szewczyk **The Breslauers**
1994, Drawing, pen, crayon on paper, 100 x 60 cm. Collection of the artist

Jacek Szewczyk **Gorale (The Mountain People)**
1993, Etching, 100 x 70 cm. Collection of the artist

Jacek Waltos **A. Chekhov -** *The Seagull*
1993, Drawing, pastel, 47 x 64.5 cm. Collection of the artist. Photograph: Marcin Limanowski

Jacek Waltos **A. Chekhov -** *Uncle Vanya* **-** Peeping at Helena
1994, Drawing, pastel, 47.5 x 64.5 cm. Collection of the artist

Ewa Zawadzka From the cycle **Czarne Pejzaze (Black Landscape) XXXIX**
1992, Print, own technique, 70 x 100 cm. Collection of the artist

Artist Biographies

Bogdan **Achimescu**

Individual Exhibitions

1992 Rathauskeller, Grebenstein, Germany
'Bezimienne', Galeria Prymat, Krakow
(with Marek Latkowski)

1993 Galerie Meier, La Chaux de Fonds,
Switzerland

1994 Galeria Il Quadrato, Chieri, Italy
Galeria Jan Fejkiel, Krakow

1995 Galeria First, Timisoara, Romania (exhibition
and performance with Jean-Jacques Locher)
Galerie Meier, La Chaux de Fonds,
Switzerland (with Elise Perret)

Group Exhibitions

1981 Studio 2, Timisoara, Romania

1990 1st International Festival of Young Artists,
Ankara, Turkey

1991 International Print Triennale, Krakow, and
Nürnberg, Germany
'Petit Format sur Papier', Musée de Petit
Format, Couvin, Belgium

1992 International Drawing Triennale, Wroclaw
Cultural Centre, Nowa Huta
'Painting, Graphics, Sculpture', Galeria Dom
Polonii, Krakow
'Ibizagrafic', International Print Biennale,
Spain

1993 International Print Exhibition, Kanagawa,
Japan
'Krakow — Cork', Crawford Municipal Art
Gallery, Cork, and Dublin, Ireland
International Print Triennial, Kochi, Japan
Premio Internazionale per l'Incisione, Biella,
Italy
International Print Triennial, Maastrict,
Holland
Prieuré de Grangourt, Switzerland
Cleveland Drawing Biennale, Great Britain
Biennale de la Societé des Amis des Arts, Le
Locle, Switzerland
Krakow Retrospective, Galeria Zacheta,
Warsaw
'Fort of Art', Krakow
'Generations', BWA Gallery, Krakow
'Ideas without Ideology', Centre for
Contemporary Art, Warsaw and Galerie Haus
Dachenröden, Erfurt, Germany

1994 Polish Print Triennale, Katowice
Wimbledon School of Art, London, Great
Britain
International Print Triennale, Krakow, and
Nürnberg, Germany
'Stone, Metal, Wood, Computer', Krakow
Expo Centre, Krakow
'Art, Science and Aesthetics', Galeria BWA,
Krakow
'Licht in Schatten', Galerie C-Keller, Weimar,
Germany
'Germinations, Europe', Breda, Holland

1995 'Germinations, Europe', Galeria Zacheta,
Warsaw
'Galerie de l'Academie', Athens, Greece and
Madrid, Spain
'3 Graphic Artists', Nordnorsk
Kunstnermuseum, Svolvaer, Norway
International Art Fair, Dresden, Germany
International Art Fair, Budapest, Hungary
'Alternative Graphics', Galeria Jan Fejkiel,
Krakow
'Krakow Meetings', BWA Gallery, Krakow
Print Biennale, Pecs, Hungary

Prizes and Awards

1990–93 Study Awards from the Polish Government,
Krakow

1993 International Print Prize, Biella, Italy

1994 Best Young Polish Artists, Myslenice, Prix ex-
Aequo
European Culture Studios, Weimar, Germany,
Working Grant Soros Foundation for an
Open Society, Award

1995 Nathaniel Salsontaal Art Fund, United States,
Study Award

Grzegorz **Banaszkiewicz**

Individual Exhibitions

1983 BWA Gallery, Czestochowa

1984 FOTO-MEDIUM-ART Gallery, Wroclaw
ON Gallery, Poznan

1988 BWA Gallery, Opole

1989 A&M Patrzyk Gallery, Czestochowa

1991 BWA Kielce, 'U JAKSY' Gallery, Miechow

1992 HADAR Gallery, Krakow

1993 Scriptoram Gallery, Ekeren, Antwerp
Maserell Centrum, Kasterlee, Belgium

Group Exhibitions

1976 International Poster Biennale, Warsaw

1978 International Drawing Triennale, Wroclaw

1979 Internationale Jugendtriennale der
Zeichnung, Nürnberg, Germany

1980 International Poster Biennale, Warsaw

1981 International Drawing Triennale, Wroclaw

1984 International Graphics Biennale/Triennale,
Krakow

1986 International Graphics Biennale/Triennale,
Krakow

1988 International Drawing Triennale, Wroclaw
International Graphics Biennale/Triennale,
Krakow
Biennale Internationale de Gravure,
Digne-les-Bains, France
International Print Biennale, Seoul, Korea

1990 Consument ART, Nürnberg, Germany

1991 International Graphics Biennale/Triennale,
Krakow
Consument ART, Nürnberg, Germany
Polish Prints, New York, United States

1992 International Drawing Triennale, Wroclaw

1994 International Graphics Biennale/Triennale,
Krakow

Intergrafia '94, World Award Winners, BWA
Gallery, Katowice
Intergrafia '94, Kultur Centrum, Ronneby,
Sweden
Intergrafia '94, Statna Gallery, Banska-
Bystrzica, Slovakia

Prizes

1976 INTERDEBIUT '76, Krakow, 2nd Prize

1981 All-Polish Graphic Contest, Lodz, 1st Prize

1986 Drawing Triennale in Memory of T.
Kulisiewicz, Kalisz, Award
All-Polish Graphic Contest in Memory of A.
Rak, Katowice, 3rd Prize

1987 10th All-Polish Graphic Contest, Lodz, Award

1989 12th All-Polish Graphic Contest, Lodz, 3rd
Prize

1989 Festival Internationale de Gravure, Menton,
France, Award

1990 INTERGRACJE '90, BWA Czestochowa, Prize

1991 All-Polish Contest, 'Czestochowa '91', 3rd
Prize

1993 Print of the Month Contest, ZPAP Krakow,
Grand Prix

1994 Print of the Month Contest, ZPAP Krakow,
Grand Prix

Works in Collections

Museum of Modern Art, Lodz
Regional Museums in Kalisz and Bydgoszcz
Kunsthalle, Nürnberg, Germany
National Library, Warsaw
BWA Galleries, Czestochowa, Loda, Opole
Maserell Centrum, Kasterlee, Belgium

Andrzej **Bebenek**

Individual Exhibitions

1977 Dom Zdrojowy, Szczawno Zdroj

1978 Galeria Maly Rynek Klubu MPiK, Krakow

1981 Srodmiejski Osrodek Kultury, Krakow

1983 BWA Gallery, Czestochowa

1985 Galeria Gologorski-Rostworowski, Krakow
Galerie in Zabo, Nuremberg, Germany
Foto Medium Art, Wroclaw Galeria
Danpolonia, Rudkobing, Denmark

1987 Galeria na Pieknej, Warsaw Galeria Arkady,
Krakow

1988 Galeria na Pietrze, Tarnobrzeg, Galeria Teatru
STU, Krakow

1989 Centar za Kulturu, Rijeka, Yugoslavia

1991 Jan Fejkiel Gallery, Krakow, Polnische
Institute, Leipzig, Germany

1994 Space Gallery, Krakow, ZPAP Gallery, Katowice

Group Exhibitions

1976 Interdebiut, Klub Pod Jaszczurami, Krakow

1977 Absolwenci, BWA Gallery, Krakow Exhibition
of Graphic Arts, Staromiejski Dom Kultury,
Warsaw
Graficy polscy i francuscy, Instytut Francuski,
Krakow

1978 7th Festival of Fine Arts, Zacheta, Warsaw

Exhibition of Contemporary Polish Drawing, Muzeum im. K. Pulaskiego, Warka
Spring Confrontations of the Young, Galeria Awangarda, BWA Gallery, Wroclaw

1979 Graficy polscy i francuscy, Instytut Francuski, Krakow
Najlepsza grafika roku, Galeria Pryzmat, Krakow
1st International Triennale of Drawing, Kunsthalle, Nuremberg, Germany
Najmlodsza grafika, Galeria ON, Poznan
Mloda grafika polska/Polish Young Graphics, Universitatsbibliothek, Kiel

1980 Exhibition of Contemporary Polish Drawing, Muzeum im. K. Pulaskiego, Warka
Stan robot, Galeria Pryzmat, Krakow
Grafik aus Polen, Staarstheater, Darmstadt, Bonn, Germany
International Graphic Biennale, Krakow
Intergrafia, International Graphic Show, BWA Gallery, Katowice
Sztuka mlodych, BWA Gallery, Lodz
Rysunki i komentarze, Muzeum Okregowe, Radom

1981 Jedenastu, Galeria Maly Rynek, Krakow
Interpretacja dziela sztuki, Galeria Pryzmat
Krakow 81, Galeria Art, Krakow
Rysunek i opis, Muzeum Okregowe, Radom
Graphic Arts at the Academy of Fine Arts in Krakow,
Ecole des Arts, Strasbourg, France
International Triennale of Drawing, Muzeum Architektury, Wroclaw
International Biennale of Graphics, Ljubljana, Yugoslavia

1983 International Biennale of Graphics, Ljubljana, Yugoslavia
Graphics in Krakow, Kunsthalle, Nuremberg, Germany
Kunstler aus Krakau, Galerie in Rathaus, Bocholt, Germany
Grafik aus Polen, Saal des Forschunginstituts der Ostfriesischen Landschaft, Aurick, Germany
Welt und Krakau, Museum Fridericianum, Kassel

1984 International Graphic Biennale, Krakow
Intergrafia, International Graphic Show, BWA Gallery, Katowice

1985 Grafika, Malarstwo, Rysunek, BWA Gallery, Zakopane

1986 Grafika z Krakowskiej ASP, Palac Sztuki, Krakow, Wroclaw, Szczecin
1st Triennale of Drawing, BWA Gallery, Kalisz
Grafik aus Krakau, Polnische Institut, Leipzig, Germany
Consument Art, Kunstmarkt, Nuremberg, Germany

1987 International Biennale of Graphics, Ljubljana, Yugoslavia
10th All-Polish Graphic Competition, BWA Gallery, Lodz

1988 International Graphic Biennale, Krakow
Intergrafia, International Graphic Show, BWA Gallery, Katowice
International Triennale of Drawing, Muzeum Architektury, Wroclaw

1989 Print from Krakow, Gerpinnes

1990 Poza obrazem, Galeria 4, BWA Gallery, Krakow
Arhus Festuge Krakow Walls, Arhus Midtby-Abent Galeri, Arhus

1991 Intergrafia, International Graphic Show, BWA Gallery, Katowice
Dotyk. Ikonografia lat 80, BWA Gallery, Krakow
1st Triennale of Polish Graphic Arts, BWA Gallery, Katowice
Jan Fejkiel Gallery Collection, Instytut Polski, Stockholm, Sweden
Pokaz wielkich obrazow Teatru STU, Kopiec Kosciuszki, Krakow

1992 Pokaz wielkich obrazow Teatru STU, Kopiec Kosciuszki, Krakow
Great Jubilee Open Salon of Painters, BWA Gallery, Krakow
10 lat pozniej, Exhibition of Contemporary Polish Drawing, Muzeum, Sztuki Wspoczesnej, Radom, Krakow, Czestochowa, Lodz
Ecole de Cracovie, Galerie des Lombards, Paris, France
Pokaz wielkich obrazow Teatru STU, EXPO '92, Seville, Spain
Miedzynarodowe nagrody polskich grafikow, Instytut Polski, Vienna, Austria, Bratislava, Czechoslovakia, and Leipzig, Wurzburg, Berlin, Germany

1993 Artysci z Krakowa, Zacheta, Warsaw
Grafika w Krakowie – Pokolenia, BWA Gallery, Krakow

1994 Art EXPO '94 International Art Fair Centre, Budapest, Hungary

Awards and Distinctions

1975 All-Polish Review of Students' Graphics, Krakow, Distinction

1978 The Best Graphic Work of the Month, Krakow, 3rd Prize
1st Triennale of the Young Drawing, Nuremberg, Germany
Grant-winning Award

1979 The Best Graphic Work of the Month (March), Krakow, 2nd Prize
The Best Graphic Work of the Month (November), Krakow, 3rd Prize

1980 The Best Graphic Work of the Month (January), Krakow, 2nd Prize
The Best Graphic Work of the Month (February), Krakow, 1st Prize

1981 The Best Graphic Work of the Month (January), Krakow, 2nd Prize
The Best Graphic Work of the Month (May), Krakow, Distinction

1991 1st Triennale of Polish Graphic Arts, Katowice, Grand Prix
The Best Graphic Work of the Month (October), Krakow, 1st Prize

Andrzej **Bednarczyk**
Individual Exhibitions

1988 Student Cultural Centre 'Rotunda', Krakow
1989 Gallery of the Academy, Krakow
Centrum, Krakow
1990 U Ambrozego, Krakow
NO TU NO, Geneva, Switzerland
1991 Stawski Gallery, Krakow

Piano Nobile, Krakow
Gallery of the Art Exposition Bureau, Lodz
1993 Stawski Gallery, Krakow
1994 Galerie '90, Bruxelles, Belgium
'Conversations with Paper', International Triennale of Graphic Art, Stawski Gallery, Krakow
1995 'Salle Capitulaire de Val Saint-Lambert', Liége, Belgium
1996 Polish Cultural Institute, London, Great Britain

Group Exhibitions

1986 'Greenbelt Festival', England, Arts Centre Group, London, Great Britain
1987 'Diploma Works '86', Lodz
5th Confrontations of the Youngest Artists from Krakow, Myslenice
1988 'Dialogue', Nurnberg, Germany
'Autumn Review of Krakow's Art', Nurnberg, Germany
1990 '58 Gallery', Chicago, United States
'Beyond the Picture', Krakow
'New Art in the Palace', Krakow
'Green Earth Festival', Legnica
'Artistes Polonaises Contemporains', Geneva, Switzerland
1991 'Dotyk/Touch: Iconography of the Eighties', BWA Gallery, Palace of Art, Krakow
International Triennale of Graphic Art, Krakow, and Nürnberg, Germany
19th International Triennale of Graphic Art, Ljubljana, Slovenia
The Krakow Art Fair, Krakow
'Bielsko Autumn', Bielsko-Biala
'Intergrafia', International Graphic Exhibition, Katowice, La Louviere, Belgium, and AFA Fair, Augsburg, Germany
'Neighbours', International exhibition, Nürnberg, Germany
'Professors of the Academy of Fine Arts', Krakow
1992 'Decouvertes '92', Grand Palais, Paris, France
5th International Drawing Triennale, Wroclaw
12th International Biennale of Woodcut, Banska Bistrica, Czechoslovakia
'Ibizagrafic '92', 12th International Biennale of Graphic Art, Spain
Yokohama International Print Auction '92, Japan
17th International Independent Exhibition of Prints, Kanagawa, Japan
1993 'Stawski Gallery Presents', International exhibition, Krakow
'Art Chicago 1993: The New Pier Show', Chicago, United States
'Inter-Kontakt-Grafik', International exhibition, Prague, Czech Republic
12th Seoul International Print Exhibition, Korea
10th International Exhibition of Graphic Art, Frechen, Germany
International Biennale of Drawing, Taiwan
'Artists from Krakow', Zacheta Gallery, Warsaw
'Generations: Graphic in Krakow', Poland
SIAC, International exhibition, Palace of Art, Krakow
'Dusseldorf Great Art Exhibition', Germany
'Polish Contemporary Graphic Art', The Polish Museum of America, Chicago, United States

1st Egyptian International Print Triennale, Giza, Egypt
2nd International Biennale of Graphic Arts, Gyor, Hungary

1994   Budapest Art Expo 1994, Hungary
'EuropArt', Geneva, Switzerland
International Graphic Art Triennale, (MTG '94), Krakow, Nürnberg, Germany
'Krakow '94', Maaltcenter, Ghent, Belgium
'Distance in Time', JIU Art Museum, Chicago, United States
'Dusseldorf Great Art Exhibition', Düsseldorf, Germany

1995   'Salon Internationale d'Art Contemporain', Strasbourg, France
'Inter-Kontakt — Grafik '95', Prague, Czech Republic
'Academy of Fine Arts in Krakow', Ronneby, Sweden
'Düsseldorf Great Art Exhibition, Düsseldorf, Germany
'Undiscovered', OKO Gallery, Chicago, United States
'Distance in Time', Museum of Art, Reno, United States
'Graphic Constellation '95', Graz, Austria
'Winners of MTG '94', BWA Gallery, Czestochowa
'Winners of MTG '94', Leipzig, Germany

1996   'Painting Exhibition', Krakow
'Art Strasbourg '96', Strasbourg, France
'Pedagodzy ASP w Krakowie', Zabrze

Awards

1987   Ministry of Culture and Art Award
Ministry of Culture and Art Scholarship
5th Confrontations of the Youngest Artists from Krakow, Myslenice Award

1988   Ministry of Culture and Art Scholarship
1991   'Bielsko Autumn', Bielsko-Biala, Award
1992   Pollock-Krasner Foundation Grant, New York United States
12th International Biennale of Woodcut, Banska Bistrica, Czechoslovakia, Honorary Award
'Ibizagrafic '92', 12th International Biennale of Graphic Art, Spain, Honorary Award
1994   International Graphic Art Triennale, Krakow, Regulation Award

Works in Collections

Urzedu Miasta, Krakow
Universal Graphic Museum, Egypt
Oxygen — Biennale Foundation
Polish Museum of America, Chicago, United States
National Gallery, Prague, Czech Republic
Museu D'Art Contemporani D'Eivissa, Spain
State Gallery, Banska Bystrica, Slovakia

Other Activities

1985   Scenography of Treasures and Nightmares, Norwid Theater, Jelenia Gora
1986   Passion, mime performance, Warsaw
1988   Loze, performance, Bialystok
1993   Artistic trip to Siberia, Russia
1994   Published book of poetry 'The Stones of My God'
Poems published in anthologies, XII Krakowska nol Poetow and Witraz-Wyspianskiemu
1995   Book of poems, The Temple of Stone, published
Poems published in anthologies Radosc and

Trwalosc Ulotnosci
1996   Poems published in anthology Jako Ptacy

Grzegorz **Bednarski**

Individual Exhibitions

1978   Galeria Eksperyment, Krakow
1980   'Wystawa malarstwa', Dworek Bialopradnicki, Krakow
1983   'Dziesiec obrazow z roku 1980', Galeria 3 obrazow ASP, Krakow
1984   Wystawa pasteli z cyklu 'Fons vitae', Galeria PAT, Krakow
'Wystawa malarstwa i rysunku' (razem z A. Walochem), BWA Gallery Zakopane
1985   'Swiadomosc tradycji' — malarstwo i rysunek, Museum Archidiecezji Warszawskiej, Warszawa
1986   Wystawa malarstwa i rysunku, Galeria Inny Swiat, Krakow
'Wystawa pasteli", Galeria Farbiarnia, Krakow
'Ni Mas Ni Menos', wystawa malarstwa, Parafia Brata Alberta, Krakow
'Czarna seria', Galeria 3 obrazow, ASP, Krakow
'Wystawa pasteli', Teatr St Witkacego, Zakopane
1988   'Wystawa malarstwa', BWA Gallery, Zakopane
1989   'Wystawa malarstwa i rysunku', Galeria SHS, Warszawa
'Wystawa malarstwa i rysunku', Galeria Gil Politechniki, Krakow
'Wystawa rysunku, pasteli i malarstwa', Galeria Teatru STU, Krakow
'Ni Mas Ni Menos', BWA Gallery, Pulawy
1990   Wystawa pasteli i rysunkow, 'Dom Misteriow', Galeria Sztuki Wspolczesnej Piotra Nowickiego, Warszawa
'Polaz malarstwa i rysunku', Galeria A. i J. Zimny, Krakow
1992   'Malarstwo', BWA Gallery, Kielce
1993   'Malarstwo', Muzeum Sztuki Wspolczesnej, Radom
'Malarstwo', Panstwowa Galeria Sztuki Wspolczesnej, Przemysl
'Malarstwo', BWA Gallery, Krosno; BWA, Bydgoszcz; BWA, Czestochowa
1994   'Wystawa malarstwa', Galeria Nad Wisla, Torun
'Wystawa malarstwa", Trybunal Koronny, Lublin

Group Exhibitions

1979   'Przestrzen Czlowieka', Galeria Pryzmat, Krakow
'Wystawa rysunku', Galeria S, Torun
1980   'Plenery 79', BWA Gallery, Krakow
'Dyplom 80', Galeria Zacheta, Warszawa
'Postawy 80', III Ogolnopolskie Konfrontacje Plastyczne, Krakow
1981   'Krakow '81', Galeria ART, Warszawa
'Absolwenci nie w BWA', Galeria Pryzmat, Krakow
'Rysunek i opis', Muzeum Okregowe, Radom
'Inspiracje dziela sztuki, inspiracja fotografia', Galeria Pryzmat, Krakow
1983   'Grafika, malarstwo, rzezba', Kamieniolom przy Kosciele sw. Jozefa, Krakow
1984   'Wystawa rysunku', Galeria Farbiarnia, Krakow
1985   'Wokol grafiki', Kosciol sw. Maksymiliana Kolbe, Krakow

'Przeciw zlu, przeciw przemocy', Kosciol sw. Maksymiliana Kolbe, Krakow
'W. strone osoby', Klasztor OO. Dominikanow, Krakow
'Droga i prawda', I Krajowa Wystawa Malarstwa Mlodych, Wroclaw
'Swiadectwo wspolnoty', Muzeum Archidiecezji Warszawskiej, Warszawa
'Niebo nowe i ziemia nowa', Parafia Milosierdzia Bozego, Warszawa
'Czas Krzyza', Kosciol Podwyzszenia Krzyza OO. Kapucynow, Bytom

1986   'Byc razem' (dedykowana J. Czapskiemu), Muzeum Archidiecezji Warszawskiej, Warszawa
'Misterium meki, smierci i zmartwychstania Pana Naszego Jezusa Chrystusa', Krypta kosciola OO. Pijarow, Krakow

1987   'Droga i prawda', Krajowe Biennale Mlodych, Wroclaw
'Wszystkie nasze dzienne sprawy', Klasztor OO. Dominikanow, Krakow
'Misterium meki smierci i zmartwychstania Jezusa Chrystusa', Kosciol Swietej Trojcy, Warszawa
'Grafika — sztuka i warsztat', BWA Gallery, Konin

1988   W kregu rysunku i grafiki', Galeria KIK, Krakow
'Szancenbach i uczniowie', BWA Krakow, Wroclaw, Warszawa, Nowy Sacz, Torun

1989   'Szancenbach i uczniowie', BWA Krakow, Wroclaw, Warszawa, Nowy Sacz, Torun
Wystawa rysunku 'Via Crucis', Galeria Inny Swiat, Krakow

1990   'Malarstwo i rysunek', Galeria A. i J. Zimny, Krakow
'Sztuka najnowsza' (wystawa A. Bonarskiego), Pawilon SARP, Warszawa

1991   '4 x B', Palac Sztuki TPSP, Krakow
'Kolekcja Duzych Obrazow', Galeria Teatru STU, Krakow, Kopiec Kosciuszki, Krakow
'Coz po artyscie w czasie marnym', Galeria Zacheta, Warszawa; Muzeum Narodowe, Krakow

1992   'Pamieci Reginy', Galeria U Kallmacha, Torun
'Natura natury', BWA Gallery, Lublin
Pracownia prof. Rodzinskiego, Galeria ASP, Krakow; Srodmiejski Osrodek Kultury, Krakow
'10 lat pozniej', wystawa polskiego rysunku wspolczesnego, Muzeum Okregowe Radom, BWA Gallery Krakow; BWA Gallery Czestochowa 93,
Panstwowa Galeria Sztuki, Lodz 1993
'Kolekcja Duzych Obrazow', Galeria Teatru STU, Kopiec Kosciuszki, Krakow
Salon Krakowski, BWA Gallery

1993   'Malarstwo, rysunek, grafika', Dominik Rostworowski Gallery, Krakow
'Malarze z Krakowa', Galeria Zacheta, Warszawa
'Malarstwo, rysunek, grafika', BWA Gallery, Krosno
'Krakowski Spleen', Galeria DAP, Warszawa
SIAC 'Sztuka miejscem odnalezienia sie', BWA Gallery, Palac Sztuki, Krakow
'Srebrny oset', Galeria u Jezuitow, Poznan
'Misterium meki i smierci Pana Jezusa', Krypta kosciola OO. Pijarow, Krakow

1991   Nagroda regulaminowa Prezydenta m.
Krakowa
Miedzynarodowe Triennale Grafiki, Krakow
5th Ogolnopolskie Quadriennale Drzeworytu,
Olsztyn, Grand Prix
Ogolnopolski konkurs graficzny, Lodz,
Wyroznienie

Works in Collections
Biblioteka Kongresu, Washington
Muzeum Sztuki Wspolczesnej, Skopje
Muzeum Sztuki, Geneva
Muzeum Narodowe, Prague
Muzeum Narodowe, Stockholm
Kunstverein, Grenchen
Miejskie Zbiory Sztuki, Dresden
Centrum Grafiki, La Louviere, Belgium
Zbiory Grafiki, Albertina, Vienna
Muzeum Narodowe, Warsaw, Krakow, Poznan
Muzeum Ziemi Bydgoskiej
Muzeum Sztuki, Lodz
Muzeum Okregowe, Torun

Zygmunt **Magner**
Selected Individual Exhibitions
1970   Painting exhibition, Modern Art Gallery,
Warsaw
1973   Painting, graphic and drawing exhibition,
DAP Gallery, Warsaw
1974   Graphic and drawing exhibition, De Kromme
Gallery, Delft, Netherlands
1975   Graphic and drawing exhibition, Kriterion
Gallery, Amsterdam, Netherlands
1976   Painting and graphic exhibition, BWA Arsenal
Gallery, Bialystok
1977   Painting, graphic and drawing exhibition, 1st
Deutsche Bank, Ludwigshafen, Germany
1979   Painting and graphic exhibition, Kordegarda,
Warsaw
1981   Painting and drawing exhibition, BWA
Gallery, Katowice
1983   Test Gallery, Warsaw
1984   Test Gallery, Warsaw
1985   Test Gallery, Warsaw
1986   Test Gallery, Warsaw
1988   Painting exhibition, BWA Gallery,
Czestochowa
Painting exhibition, Arkady Gallery, Krakow
1989   Painting and drawing exhibition, Slaski
Muzeum, Katowice
1990   Painting exhibition in Historics of Art Gallery,
Krakow
1991   Painting, graphic and drawing exhibition,
Hartmanstrasse 45 Gallery, Ludwigshafen,
Germany

Selected Group Exhibitions
1968   2nd Festival of Art, Warsaw
4th Festival of Painting, Szczecin
1969   4th Polish Exhibition of Graphic Art, Warsaw
Exhibition of Polish Graphic Art, Skopje,
Sarajevo, Bosnia-Herzegovina, Yugoslavia
1970   3rd Festival of Art, Sopot
1971   3rd Triennale of Drawing, Wroclaw
5th Polish Exhibition of Graphic Art, Poznan
1972   4th Festival of Art, Warsaw
1973   Exhibition of Polish Art, Mannheim, Germany
Exhibition of Polish Graphic Art, Algiers,
Algeria
1974   5th Festival of Art, Warsaw

Exhibition of Polish Graphic Art, Rabat, Tunis
1975   'Romantyzm I Romantycznoscw Sztuce
Polskiej XIX i XX wieku', Warsaw, Katowice
1976   Exhibition of Polish Graphic Art, Tunis
7th Polish Graphic Art Exhibition, Warsaw
'W Kregu Metafory', Warsaw
6th Festival of Art, Warsaw
6th International Graphic Biennale, Krakow
1977   Exhibition of Polish Graphic Art, Rotenburg,
Germany
Exhibition of Polish Graphic Art, Clermont-
Ferrand, France
1978   7th Festival of Art, Warsaw
'Prawda Czlowieka Prawda Artysy', Wroclaw
5th International Triennale of Drawing,
Wroclaw
1979   18th International Joan Miro Drawing
Competition, Barcelona, Spain
Exhibition of Polish Graphic Art, Oslo,
Norway
Exhibition of Polish Graphic Art,
Ludwigshafen, Germany
'Rysunek dzielo spelnione', Warsaw
1980   19th International Joan Miro Drawing
Competition, Barcelona, Spain
'Druk Plaski', Warsaw
1981   Exhibition of Polish Graphic Art, Osaka, Japan
Exhibition of Polish Graphic Art, Lisbon,
Portugal
Exhibition of Polish Graphic Art, Cairo, Egypt
Exhibition of Polish Graphic Art, Algiers,
Algeria
9th Polish Exhibition of Graphic Art, Warsaw
Festival of Art, Warsaw
1982   6th International Biennale of Painting,
Koszyce
Exhibition of Polish Art, Budapest, Hungary
'Granica Marzen I Wyobrazni', Sofia, Bulgaria
1983   Exhibition of Polish Art, Prague,
Czechoslovakia
Exhibition of Polish Painting, Varrelbusch,
Germany
1985   Exhibition of Polish Art, Gent, Belgium
Exhibition of Polish Modern Painting, Beijing,
Xian, Czenage, China
1988   Exhibition of Polish Art, Berlin, Germany
1991   'Memory and its Differents Aspects',
Bruxelles, Belgium
1992   Polish Graphic Art exhibition, Istanbul,
Turkey
'Warsaws' Akademy Artists', Ludwigshafen,
Germany
1994   'W kregu Nowej Figuracji', Warsaw
1995   'Time, Perspective, Matter, Object'.(with
Henryk Gostynski, Julian Raczko and Gunther
Wilhelm), DAP Gallery, Warsaw, and
Kunstverein, Ludwigshafen, Germany
Painting exhibition (with Julian Raczko),
Batuz Foundation Gallery, Altzella, Germany

Awards
1974   5th Festival of Art, Warsaw, First Prize and
Gold Medal
1982   6th International Biennale of Painting,
Koszyce, Award

Works in Public Collections
National Museum, Warsaw
Slaski Museum, Katowice
City Museum, Katowice
National Museums, Gdansk, Przemysl

Art Centre 'Studio', Warsaw
National Library, Warsaw
National Gallery, Washington, United States
Lincoln University Museum, Nebraska, United States
Also in private collections in Poland and abroad

Jan **Mlodozeniec**
Selected Individual Exhibitions
1962   Kordegarda Gallery, Warsaw
1963   Galerie in der Biberstrasse, Vienna, Austria
1966   Osrodek Kultury Polskiej, Prague,
Czechoslovakia
1968   Galeria Sztuki, Poitiers, France
1969   Galeria Grafiki Klubu MPiK 'Ruch', Lublin
Dom Artysty Plastyka, Warsaw
1971   Muzeum Ziemi Przemyskiej, Przemysl
1975   Brno, Czechoslovakia
1978   Galerie am Prater, Berlin, Germany
Dom Artysty Plastyka, Warsaw
1980   BWA Gallery, Bialystok
1981   Polish Institute, Stockholm, Sweden
BWA Gallery, Zamosc
1983   Lahti Museum, Finland
1984   Muzeum Plakatu Wilanow, Warsaw
1985   La Salle, Italy
1986   BWA Gallery, Zakopane
Galeria Mlodych, Warsaw
Galeria Teatru Nowego, Warsaw
1988   Polski Osrodek Kultury i Informacji, Lipsk
1989   Polski Osrodek Kultury i Informacji,
Budapest, Hungary
Polish Bookshop, Paris, France
1991   Deutsches Plakat Museum, Essen, Germany
Galerie von Oertzen, Frankfurt, Germany
Creation Gallery G8, Tokyo, Japan
1992   Galeria Grafiki i Plakatu, Warsaw
1993   Muzeum Okregowe, Sandomierz
Venthonne, Switzerland
BWA Galeria Design, Wroclaw
Galeria Sztuki Wspolczesnej, Ostrow Wlk
Galeria Ksiegarnia Cztelnik, Warsaw
1994   Polish Cultural Institute, Berlin, Germany
Muzeum X. Dunikowskiego, Warsaw
1995   Galerie Espace Ambuel, Sion, Switzerland
Galerie Bernauer III, Berlin, Germany

Selected Awards
1955   International Exhibition of Young Artists,
Warsaw, Silver Medal
1963   Zielona Gora, 'Zlotego Grona' Medal
1965   International Book Exhibition, Lipsk, Silver
Medal
1966   2nd Biennale Grafiki Uzytkowej, Brno,
Czechoslovakia, Silver Medal
1967   Ministry of Culture, 3rd Prize for Posters
1971   4th Biennale of Polish Posters, Katowice, Silver
Medal
1973   Exhibition of Book Graphics, Warsaw, 2nd
Prize
1977   7th Biennale of Polish Posters, Katowice,
Bronze Medal
1980   8th Biennale of Polish Posters, Katowice, Gold
Medal
1981   9th Biennale of Polish Posters, Katowice, Gold
Medal
9th Biennale of Polish Posters, Katowice,
Bronze Medal
1983   5th Biennale of Posters, Lahti, Finland, 1st
Prize

1985   11th Biennale of Polish Posters, Katowice, Honorary Medal
1989   Warsaw, Poster of the Year Award

Works in Collections
Poster Museum, Wilanow, Warsaw
National Museum, Poznan
Bibliotheque Forney, Paris, France
Kunstgewerbe Museum, Zurich, Switzerland
Deutsches Plakat Museum, Essen, Germany
Ladhen Taidemuseo, Lahti, Finland
Stedlijk Museum, Amsterdam, Netherlands
Israel Museum, Jerusalem, Israel
Dansk Plakatmuseum, Aarhus, Denmark

Selected Bibliography
Alain le Quernec, 'Novum Gebrauchsgraphic 9', 'The Poster Designer Jan Mlodozeniec', 1984
E. Kruszewska, 'Graphis 236', 1985
N. Matsuura, 'Creation 7', Tokyo, 1990
The Thames and Hudson Encyclopaedia of Graphic Design
and Designers, Thames and Hudson, London, 1992
'Idea 240', Tokyo, 1993
Who's Who in Graphic Art, Benteli-Werd Verlags AG, Zurich, 1994
K. Dydo, 100th Anniversary of Polish Poster Art, Krakow, 1994
40th Anniversary Special Edition, '100 Graphic Designers of the World', BWA Gallery Krakow, 1994
'Muzeum Ulicy — Plakat Polski w Kolekcji Muzeum Plakatu w Wilonowie', Krupski i Ska, Warsaw, 1996

Marian **Nowinski**

Selected Individual Exhibitions
1980   BWA Gallery, Torun
1981   Municipal Gallery, Picassent, Spain
1982   Municipal Gallery, Stanze del Convento di San Paulo, Parma, Italy
1983   Italian Cultural Institute, Warsaw
1985   Test Gallery, Warsaw
1987   Galerie Maison des Arts, Clermont-Ferrand, France
1989   Dresdner Bank, Herford, Germany
1992   Centre Culturel Valeri Larbuad, Vichy, France
1993   Municipal Gallery, Lohne, Germany
1994   Poster & Graphic Gallery, Warsaw
1995   Gallery '90', Szczecin
           Zapiecek Gallery, Warsaw
1996   Test Gallery, Warsaw
           Municipal Gallery, Genoa, Italy

Selected Prizes and Awards
1976   Miedzynarodowy Instytut Praw Czlowieka, Strasbourg, France, 2nd Nagroda za plakat
1977   Ogolnopolska wystawa malarstwa i rysunku, Chorzow, 1st Nagroda
1978   Nagroda Miedzynarodowego Komitetu Pokoju za plakat, 7th Miedzynarodowe Biennale Plakatu, Warsaw
           Miedzynarodowy konkurs na plakat Swiatowego Festiwalu Mlodziezy i Studentow, Budapest, 2nd Nagroda za plakat
1979   Iraqi Cultural Centre, London, 2nd and 3rd Nagroda oraz srebrny medal za plakat
           8th Biennale Plakatu Polskiego, Katowice, 1st Nagroda i zloty medal za plakat
1980   Nagroda specjalna Ogolnopolskiego Komitetu Pokoju za plakat, 8th Miedzynarodowe Biennale Plakatu, Warsaw

1987   2nd Nagroda Miedzynarodowego Jury PALMARES za plakat, 2nd Miedzynarodowy Salon Plakatu, Grand Palais, Paris
1988   Wyroznienie 'Indywidualnosc roku 1987' za plakat przyznane przez Klub Kolekcjonerow Plakatu
           Miedzynarodowe Triennale Rysunku, Wroclaw, srebrny medal za rysunek
           Nagroda specjalna Pracowni Sztuk Plastycznych, 12th Miedzynarodowe Biennale Plakatu, Warszawa

Works in Collections
Muzeum Plakatu w Wilanowie
Muzeum Okregowego w Bialej Podlaskie
CBWA 'Zacheta', Warsaw
Museo Internacional da la Resitencia Salvator Allende w Havana, Cuba
Ayuntamiento de Picassent, Spain
Works in private collections in Denmark, Finland, France, Great Britain, Italy, Spain, Germany, United States and Poland

Tadeusz **Nuckowski**

Selected Individual Exhibitions
1976   Galeria Kalambur, Wroclaw
1977   Galeria Desa, Przemysl
1984   Cuts Gallery, London, Great Britain
1985   Muzeum Narodowe, Przemysl
1986   Galeria Maly Rynek, Krakow (towarzyszaca 11 MBG)
           Galeria Kordegarda, Warsaw
1989   BWA Gallery, Torun
1990   Norske Grafikere Gallery, Oslo, Norway
1992   Galeria Balucka, BWA Gallery, Lodz
1993   Panstwowa Galeria Sztuki Wspolczesnej, Przemysl
1994   Galeria Jan Fejkiel, Krakow

Selected Group Exhibitions
1976   Ogolnopolska Wystawa Sztuki Mlodych, Sopot
           Interdebiut '76, Krakow (wystawa towarzyszaca 7 MGB)
1977   Absolwenci 1974–76, BWA Gallery, Krakow
1978   8th Ogolnopolska Wystawa Grafiki, Warsaw
           Osmiu Grafikow z Polski, Fundacja Kosciuszkowska, New York, United States
1979   2nd Quadriennale Drzeworytu i Linorytu Polskiego, Olsztyn
           2nd Ogolnopolski Konkurs Graficzny im. J. Gielniaka, Jelenia Gora
1980   8th Miedzynarodowe Biennale Grafiki, Krakow
           Laureaci Krakowskich Biennale, Instytut Kultury Polskiej, London, Great Britain
1981   14th Miedzynarodowe Biennale Grafiki, Ljubljana, Yugoslavia
           3rd Ogolnopolski Konkurs Graficzny im. J. Gielniaka, Jelenia Gora
1983   Dialouge Grave, Miedzynarodowe Triennale Grafiki, Spa, Belgium
           4th Ogolnopolski Konkurs Graficzny im. J. Gielniaka, Jelenia Gora
1984   10th Miedzynarodowe Biennale Grafiki, Krakow
           Intergrafia, Katowice
           XYLON 9, Poland, Switzerland, Germany, Italy
           6th Biennale Europeene de la Gravure, Mulhouse, France
           9th Miedzynarodowa Wystawa Rysunku, Rijeka, Yugoslavia

1985   International Day Art I, Budapest, Hungary
           5th Ogolnopolski Konkurs Graficzny im. J. Gielniaka, Jelenia Gora
1986   Prints From All Over, Boulder, Colorado, United States
           Bois Pluriel 2 — Miedzynarodowe Biennale Drzeworytu, Evry, France
           11th Miedzynarodowe Biennale Grafiki, Krakow
           Consument Art, Nürnberg, Germany
           Polski druk wypukly, Schwetzingen, St. Blasien, Germany
1987   Graphica Atlantica, Reykjavik, Iceland
           XYLON 10, Switzerland, Poland, Germany, France, Italy
           Grafica Polacca Contemporanea, Milan, Italy
           Z kregu Humberta, grafika z krakowskiej ASP, Wroclaw, Szczecin
           4th Quadriennale Drzeworytu i Linorytu Polskiego, Olsztyn
1988   12th Miedzynarodowe Biennale Grafiki, Krakow
           Intergrafia, Katowice
           California Society of Printmakers, Membership Show, Menlo Park, United States
           3rd Annual International Exhibition of Miniature Art, Toronto, Canada
1989   Polish Prints: A Contemporary Graphic Tradition, Lincoln, St Louis, Philadelphia, Chicago, Clark, United States
           California Society of Printmakers, Danish Exchange Show, Odense, Denmark
           2nd Festival International de Gravure, Menton, France
           Grafika z Krakowskiej ASP, Chatelet, Belgium
           Petit format de papier, Cul-des-Sarts, Belgium
1990   XYLON 11, Switzerland, Italy, Germany, Belgium
           Premio Internazionale Biella per l'Incisione, Biella, Italy
           Intergrafik '90, Berlin, Germany
           Art of Today III, Budapest, Hungary
1991   5th International Biennale Print Exhibit, Taipei, Taiwan
1992   JETZT (teraz), Polnische Graphik der Gegenwart, Vienna, Austria
           Wystawa Grafiki Polskiej, Akademia Sztuki, Moscow, Russia
           Contemporary Relief Print, Texas City, United States
           2nd Bienal Internacional de Grabado, Orense, Spain
1993   Polnische Graphik in der Albertina, Vienna, Austria
           XYLON 12, Winterthur, Switzerland
           2nd International Biennale of Graphic Arts, Gyor, Hungary
           Triennale Polskiego Rysunku Wspolczesnego, Lubaczow
           1st Internationale Grafiek Biennale, Maastricht, Netherlands
1994   2nd Triennale Grafiki Polskiej, Katowice
           Cztery zywioly wspolczesnej grafiki polskiej, Krakow

Awards
1976   Interdebiut '76, Krakow, Druga nagroda regulaminowa (second regular prize)
1979   w Konkursach Graficznych im. J. Gielniaka, Jelenia Gora, Wyroznienie (honourable mention)

2nd Quadriennale Drzeworytu i Linorytu Polskiego, Olsztyn, Trzecia nagroda (third prize)

1980 8th Miedzynarodowe Biennale Grafiki, Krakow, Trzecia nagroda regulaminowa (third regular prize)

1981 w Konkursach Graficznych im. J. Gielniaka, Jelenia Gora, Wyroznienie (honourable mention)

Works in Collections

Victoria and Albert Museum, London, Great Britain
Graphische Sammlung Albertina, Vienna, Austria
Centre de la Gravure et de l'Image Imprimee, La Louviere, Belgium
Panstwowa Galeria Sztuki, Lodz
Muzea Narodowe in Szczecin and Przemysl

Ryszard Otreba

Selected Individual Exhibitions

1963 Galeria Pegaz, Zakopane
1966 Galeria Domu Pracy Tworczej, Erfurt, Germany
1967 Kurzband House, New York, United States
1969 Biuro Wystaw Artystycznych, Zakopane
1970 Galeria ZPAP 'Sien gdanska', Gdansk
   Klub Dziennikarzy 'Pod gruszka', Krakow
1973 Biuro Wystaw Artystycznych, Krakow
   Biuro Wystaw Artystycznych, Gdynia
1975 PRO, Charlottenborg, Denmark
   Galery Art Center 1890, Venlo, Netherlands
   Galeria 'B', Krakow
1977 Kjarvalsstodum, Reykjavik, Iceland
1979 LK Galerie, Varrelbusch, Germany
   Biuro Wystaw Artystycznych, Zakopane
   Galeria Maly Rynek, Krakow
1980 Galeria DESA, Przemysl
1981 Stadia Graphics Gallery, Sydney, Australia
1982 Hawthorn City Art Gallery, Melbourne, Australia
1983 Galerie in Zabo, Nürnberg, Germany
   City Art Gallery, Uddevalla, Sweden
1984 Artists Space, Melbourne, Australia
1985 Allegro Gallery, Sydney, Australia
   Centrum Kultury Polskiej, Sofia, Bulgaria
1986 Galeria DESA, Krakow
   LK Galerie, Varrelbusch, Germany
1987 Grona Paletten, Stockholm, Sweden
   ZiF Galerie, Bielefeld, Germany
1988 Salon Sztuki Wspolczesnej, Lodz
   Galeria Sztuki Wspolczesnej, Cieszyn
   Art Gallery, Funasdalen, Sweden
   Biuro Wystaw Artystycznych, Bielsko-Biala
   Place Hymiee, Gerpinnes, Belgium
   Luigi Marrozzini Gallery, San Juan, Puerto Rico
   Biuro Wystaw Artystycznych, Torun
1989 Link Gallery, Rochester, United States
   The Blue Sky Art Gallery, Pittsburg, United States
1990 Galerie Michel Vokaer, Bruxelles, Belgium
1991 Galerie Kunen, Dülmen, Germany
   Atrium Gallery, Storrs, United States
   RISD Gallery, Providence, United States
1992 Pawilon Wystawowy BWA, Krakow
   Mala Galeria Grafiki, Lublin
   Zimmergalerie, Iserlohn, Germany
1993 SPICCHI dell'EST srl. Galeria d'Arte, Rome, Italy

Kunsthaus Pinx, Bochum, Germany
Galeria Sztuki Wspolczesnej, Opole

Group Exhibitions

1966 International Print Biennale/Triennale, Krakow
1968 International Print Biennale/Triennale, Krakow
   British International Print Biennale, Bradford, Great Britain
1969 Biennale Internationale de la Gravure, Liege, Belgium
1970 International Print Biennale/Triennale, Krakow
   International Poster Biennale, Warszawa
1971 Premi Internacional Dibuix Joan Miro, Barcelona, Spain
1972 International Print Biennale/Triennale, Krakow
   British International Print Biennale, Bradford, Great Britain
   International Poster Biennale, Warszawa
   Biennale internazionale della Grafica d'Arte, Firenze, Italy
1973 British International Drawing Biennale, Middlesbrough, Great Britain
   Premi Internacional Dibuix Joan Miro, Barcelona, Spain
1974 International Print Biennale/Triennale, Krakow
   British International Print Biennale, Bradford, Great Britain
   Biennale Internationale d'Art, Menton, France
   Premi Internacional Dibuix Joan Miro, Barcelona, Spain
   La Bienal, Ibiza, Spain
   Biennale Mobile, Edinburgh, Great Breat Britain
   Intergrafia, Katowice
1975 Premi Internacional Dibuix Joan Miro, Barcelona, Spain
1976 International Print Biennale/Triennale, Krakow
   British International Print Biennale, Bradford, Great Britain
   Biennale Internationale d'Art, Menton, France
   Premi Internacional Dibuix Joan Miro, Barcelona, Spain
   XYLON Int. Trienale Exhibition of Wood Engraving, Winterthur, Switzerland
   Exposition Int. de Gravure, Condé-Bonsecours, Belgium
   Norwegian International Print Biennale/Triennale, Fredrikstad, Norway
   Internationale Grafik Biennale, Frechen, Germany
1977 International Biennale of Graphic Art, Ljubljana,Yugoslavia
1978 International Print Biennale/Triennale, Krakow
   Premi Internacional Dibuix Joan Miro, Barcelona, Spain
   La Bienal, Ibiza, Spain
   Exposition Int. de dessins originaux, Rijeka, Yugoslavia
   International Drawing Triennale, Wroclaw
   Intergrafia, Katowice
1979 British International Print Biennale, Bradford, Great Britain

Premi Internacional Dibuix Joan Miro, Barcelona, Spain
   XYLON Int. Triennale Exhibition of Wood Engraving, Winterthur, Switzerland
   International Biennale of Graphic Art, Ljubljana, Yugoslavia
   Biennale of European Graphic Arts, Heidelberg, Germany
   Premio Internazionale Biella per l'Incisione, Biella, Italy
1980 International Print Biennale/Triennale, Krakow
   International Poster Biennale, Warszawa
   Premi Internacional Dibuix Joan Miro, Barcelona, Spain
   Norwegian International Print Biennale/Triennale, Fredrikstad, Norway
   Exposition Int. de dessins originaux, Rijeka, Yugoslavia
   Premio Internazionale Biella per l'Incisione, Biella, Italy
   Miami International Print Biennale, Miami, Florida, United States
   International Graphic Art Exhibition, Linz, Austria
1981 International Biennale of Graphic Art, Ljubljana, Yugoslavia
   International Drawing Triennale, Wroclaw
1982 British International Print Biennale, Bradford, Great Britain
1983 XYLON Int. Triennale Exhibition of Wood Engraving, Winterthur, Switzerland
   Premio Internazionale Biella per l'Incisione, Biella, Italy
   Biennale int. de gravure sur bois, de Croissy-sur-Seine, France
   Int. Biennale-Petit format de papier, Cul-des-Sarts, Couvin, Belgium
   Triennale Int. de Gravure-Dialoque grave, Spa, Belgium
   World Print Triennale, San Francisco, California, United States
   Prints from Blocks: Gaugin to now, New York, United States
1984 International Print Biennale/Triennale, Krakow
   Norwegian International Print Biennale/Triennale, Fredrikstad, Norway
   Exposition Int. de dessins originaux, Rijeka, Yugoslavia
   Biennale MPAC Print Acquisitive, Mornington, Victoria, Australia
   International Prints & Illustrated Books, Canberra, ACT, Australia
   Intergrafia, Katowice
1985 Premi Internacional Dibuix Joan Miro, Barcelona, Spain
1986 International Print Biennale/Triennale, Krakow
   Norwegian International Print Biennale/Triennale, Fredrikstad, Norway
   Exposition Int. de dessins originaux, Rijeka, Yugoslavia
   Intergrafia, Katowice
1987 XYLON Int. Triennale Exhibition of Wood Engraving, Winterthur, Switzerland
   Int. Biennale-Petit format de papier, Cul-des-Sarts, Couvin, Belgium
   International Drawing Triennale, Kalisz

1988   International Print Biennale/Triennale, Krakow
     International Drawing Triennale, Wroclaw
     Intergrafia, Katowice
     International Print Biennale, Seoul, Korea

1989   Norwegian International Print Biennale/Triennale, Fredrikstad, Norway
     International Print Biennale, Varna, Bulgaria
     L'Europe des Graveurs, Grenoble, France
     Int. Independent Exhibition of Prints, Kanagawa, Japan

1991   International Print Biennale/Triennale, Krakow
     Intergrafia, Katowice

1992   Norwegian International Print Biennale/Triennale, Fredrikstad, Norway
     International Drawing Triennale, Wroclaw
     Baltic Countries Graphic Art Triennale, Gdansk

1993   International Biennale of Graphic Art, Ljubljana, Slovenia
     Internationale Grafiek Biennale, Maastricht, Netherlands
     Graphic Arts Contest 'Ostblick-Westblick, Austria
     Egyptian International Print Triennale, Giza, Egypt

1994   International Print Biennale/Triennale, Krakow
     Intergrafia, Katowice

Prizes and Awards

1971   International Print Biennale, Krakow, Special prize
     Polish Drawing Triennale, Wroclaw, 1st Prize

1975   Polish Print Exhibition, Lodz, 2nd Prize

1978   International Print Biennale, Krakow, Special Prize
     International Exhibition of Original Drawings, Rijeka, Yugoslavia, Special Prize

1979   Polish Print Exhibition, Lodz, 1st prize
     Polish Quadriennale of Woodcut, Olsztyn, 2nd Prize

1980   International Print Biennale, Krakow, 2nd Prize
     International Exhibition of Original Drawings, Rijeka, Yugoslavia, Special Prize

1989   Polish Print Exhibition, Jelenia Gora, 3rd Prize
     International Print Biennale, Varna, Bulgaria, Award

1991   Polish Print Triennale, Katowice, Special Prize
     Polish Quadriennale of Woodcut, Olsztyn, Special Award

1993   Polish Contemporary Drawing Triennale, Lubaczow, Special Prize

1995   Polish Quadriennale of Woodcut, Olsztyn, Grand Prix

Henryk **Ozog**

Selected Individual Exhibitions

1985   Galeria 3 Obrazow, ASP, Krakow
     Galeria Grafiki i Plakatu, DESA, Warsaw

1987   Galeria Rencontre d'Espaces, Strasbourg, France
     Galeria 72, Poznan

1988   Galeria Inny Swiat, Krakow
     Galerie Du Club 44, La Chaux de Fonds, Switzerland

1989   Intaglio Printmaker Gallery, Melbourne, Australia

1990   Galeria A, Stary Rynek, Poznan
     Galleri Heden, Goteborg, Sweden

1991   Galeria GP, Warsaw
     Galeria Balucka, BWA Gallery, Lodz
     La Baumatte, La Chaux de Breuleux, Switzerland

Selected Group Exhibitions

1984   Miedzynarodowe Biennale Grafiki, Krakow
     2nd Triennale Europea de l'Incisione, Venice, Italy

1985   Polish Prints at World Print Council, San Francisco, United States
     4th Europaischen Grafik Biennale, Baden Baden, West Germany
     Boulder UMC Fine Arts Center, University of Colorado, United States

1986   Miedzynarodowe Biennale Grafiki, Krakow
     Polish Prints from Krakow, Atrium Gallery, Storrs, United States

1987   Premio Internazionale per Biella l'Incisione, Biella, Italy

1988   Miedzynarodowe Biennale Grafiki, Krakow
     Actuele Poolse Schilderkunst, Brunssum, Netherlands

1989   Polish Prints, A Contemporary Graphic Tradition Lincoln, United States

1990   FIAC, Grand Palais, Paris, France
     Miedzynarodowe Biennale Grafiki, Frechen, Germany
     Kunstler aus Krakau, Galerie Signe, Aachen, Germany

1991   Targi Sztuki SAGA, Grand Palais, Paris, France
     Miedzynarodowe Triennale Grafiki, Krakow
     Miedzynarodowe Triennale Grafiki, Lubljana, Slovenia
     Jan Fejkiel Gallery Collection, Instytut Kultury Polskiej, Stockholm, Sweden

1992   Wspolczesna Grafika Polska, Retretti, Finland
     LINEART, Gandawa, Belgium
     Sztuka w Europie 1992, France, Poland, Bad Kissingen, Germany

1993   Portret ironiczny, BWA i Jan Fejkiel Gallery, Krakow
     Grafik aus Krakow, Galerie Junge Kunst, Frankfurt, Germany
     Contemporary Art–Art Multiple, Düsseldorf, Germany

Jan **Pamula**

Selected Individual Exhibitions

1968   La Scala Gallery, Rome, Italy

1971   Polish Cultural Institute, London, Great Britain
     Zaydler Gallery, London, Great Britain

1973   Arkady Gallery, Krakow

1977   BWA Gallery, Lodz

1978   Hungarian Artists Gallery, Pecs, Hungary

1979   'Out' Gallery, Gdansk
     Project Studio One, New York, United States

1980   Institut Polonais, Paris, France
     Desa Gallery, Krakow
     BWA Gallery, Opole

1981   Krzysztofory Gallery, Krakow

1982   The Kosziuszko Foundation, New York, United States
     Maria Hagadus Studio Gallery, Bedford Hills, United States

1984   Black Gallery, Krakow

1986   '72 Gallery', Chelm Museum, Chelm

1987   '72 Gallery', Chelm Museum, Chelm
     Foyer Gallery, Darmstadt, Germany
     'Actual Art' Gallery, Krakow
     Silesian University Gallery, Cieszyn

1992   Atrium Gallery, UCONN, Storrs, United States

1993   Culture Centre, Kamienica Lamellich, Krakow

1994   Windows Gallery, NYIT, New York, United States
     Rotunda Gallery at the Kosziuszko Foundation, New York, United States
     Aspekty Gallery, Warsaw

Selected Group Exhibitions

1970   International Print Biennale, Musee d'Art Moderne, Paris, France

1970   International Print Biennale, Krakow

1974   International Biennal of Contemporary Art, Menton, France

1976   International Print Biennale, Krakow

1978   'Geometry and Emotion', Geometric Tendencies in the Printmaking of the 20th Century, National Museum, Warsaw

1980   Artists Grantee of the French Government, UNESCO, Paris, France

1981   International Biennale of Contemporary Art, Brest, France

1982   British International Print Biennale, Bradford, Great Britain
     8th International Print Exhibition, Kanagawa, Japan
     'From Winslow Homer to Robert Rauschenberg', Exhibition of Prints, Pratt Graphic Center Gallery, New York, United States

1984   'World and Krakow', International Print Exhibition, Museum Fridericianum, Kassel, Germany

1985   'Art and Geometry', Exhibitions accompanying a series of international symposiums on art and geometry, 72 Gallery, Chelm

1986   International Print Biennale, Krakow

1989   2nd International Print Festival 'East-European Printmaking', Menton, France

1991   International Print Triennale, Krakow

1992   Computer Graphics in Fine Arts, State Gallery, Banska Bystrica; Medium Gallery, Bratislava, Slovakia

1993   Computer Graphics in Fine Arts, State Gallery, Banska Bystrica; Medium Gallery, Bratislava, Slovakia
     New York Digital Salon, Art Directors Club, New York, United States

1994   International Print Triennale, Krakow
     1st International Print Triennale 'Colour in Graphic Art', Torun

1995   'Art and Geometry', Exhibitions accompanying a series of international symposiums on art and geometry, 72 Gallery, Chelm

Works in Collections

Albertina Graphische Sammlung, Vienna, Austria
Portland Art Museum, Oregon, United States
The Kosziuszko Foundation, New York, United States
Victoria and Albert Museum, London, Great Britain
National Museum, Warsaw
National Museum, Krakow
Museum of Auschwitz Concentration Camp

Leon Wyczolkowski Museum, Bydgoszcz
Regional Museums in Poland — Szczecin, Chelm,
Bytom, Lublin
Museum of Architecture, Wroclaw
Jagiellonian Library Print Collection, Krakow

Marcin **Pawlowski**
Individual Exhibitions
1988   University Gallery, Cieszyn
1989   Gallery of Fine Arts Academy, Krakow
1992   Miejsce Gallery, Cieszyn
1994   5A Gallery, Krakow
1995   Literatur Werkstatt, Berlin, Germany
Selected Group Exhibitions
1981   'Krakow '81', Warsaw
1985   3rd International Triennale of Drawing,
        Nürnberg, West Germany
1986   1st International Triennale of Drawing, Kalisz
1987   2nd International Biennale of Architecture,
        Krakow
1988   4th International Triennale of Drawing,
        Wroclaw
        '4 X Bronowice Nowe', Photo exhibition,
        ZPAF Gallery, Krakow
1989   'Thoughts Moving, Parallel Actions', Warsaw
1992   5th International Triennale of Drawing, Wroclaw
        'Ten Years Later', Radom
1993   'Coordinates', Krakow
        'Fort of Art', Krakow
1994   'Fort of Art', Krakow
1995   '+RAUM', Parochialkirche, Berlin, Germany
        '10th Krakovian Meetings — Free Town of
        Krakow', Krakow
        'Order', Zakopane
1996   'Order 2', Krakow

Janusz **Przybylski**
Selected Individual Exhibitions
1970   Zacheta Gallery, Warsaw
1973   Sculpture Gallery, Warsaw
        Malmo, Sweden
1974   Wartheim Gallery, Berlin, Germany
1975   Düsseldorf, Germany
1977   Düsseldorf, Germany
1978   Zacheta Gallery, Warsaw
        BWA Gallery, Lodz
1980   Studio Art Gallery, Warsaw
        Cologne, Germany
1985   Studio Art Gallery, Warsaw
1986   BWA Gallery, Lodz
1987   Test Gallery, Warsaw
        Kordegarda Gallery, Warsaw
        Düsseldorf, Germany
Group Exhibitions
Participated in many international and overseas
exhibitions:
1st, 2nd, 3rd and 6th International Biennale of
Graphic Art, Krakow
Moderne Polask Maleri, Norway; Finland; Denmark
Biennale of the Young, Paris
'Contemporary Polish Graphic Arts', Havana, Cuba
International Biennale of Graphic Art in Bradford,
Great Britain, Heidelberg, Germany, Frechen,
Germany, Ljubljana, Slovenia and Liege, Belgium
Awards
1967   Internationale Ausstellung Graphic,
        Vienna, 1st Prize

1968   1st All-Poland Contest for a work of
        Graphic Art, Lodz, 1st Prize
1970   Third Festival of Fine Arts,
        Warsaw, Silver Medal
1971   11th Biennale of Art, Sao Paulo, Gold Medal
1972   6th Festival of Contemporary
        Painting, Szczecin, Grand Prix
1973   4th Festival of Fine Arts, Warsaw, Gold Medal
        1st Triennale of Painting and Graphic Arts,
        Lodz, Ministry of Culture and Art Award
1976   Section 'Woman', 7th All-Poland Exhibition
        of Graphic Arts, Warsaw, 1st Prize
1985   Talla, Italy, 'Apollo '85' Medal
1986   Ministry of Culture and Art Award, 2nd
        degree
1987   'Miniature '87', Bydgoszcz, Grand Prix
Works in Collections
National Museum, Warsaw
National Library, Warsaw
Cabinet of Prints, Albertina, Vienna
Bibliotheque Nationale, Paris
Tate Gallery, London
Also in private collections in Poland and abroad

Leszek **Rozga**
Individual Exhibitions
Since 1954 has had more than 150 individual
exhibitions in Lodz, Warsaw, Wroclaw, Torun,
Katowice, Poznan, Bydgoszcz, Lublin, Koszalin and
Bialystok in Poland
Hamburg, Koln, Nürnberg, Bremen and Berlin,
Germany
Vienna, Austria
Oslo, Norway
London, Great Britain
Paris, France
Prague, Czech Republic
Barcelona, Spain
Rome, Italy
New York and Chicago, United States
Group Exhibitions
Since 1954 has participated in over 500 group
exhibitions in Poland and many other countries
Awards
Has received over 60 Awards and Honorary Diplomas
including:
1971   Polish Ministry of Culture and Art, 2nd Class
        Award
1981   Polish Ministry of Culture and Art, 1st Class
        Award
1985   City of Lodz, Artistic Award
1994   Polish Ministry of Culture and Art, Individual
        Award, First Class
Works in Collections
Muzeum Narodowe, Warsaw, Krakow, Gdansk, Poznan,
Szczecin
Bibliotheque National, Paris, France
Graphotek, Bremen, Germany
Graphotek, Erlangen, Germany
Graphotek, Oldenburg, Germany
Pushkin Museum, Moscow, Russia
Hermitage Museum, St Petersburg, Russia
Also in private collections in Australia, France, Spain,
Germany, Switzerland, the United States and Italy
Bibliography
I. Jakimowicz, Contemporary Polish Graphic Art, Arkady
Publishers, Warsaw, 1963
H. Anders, Leszek Rozga, Graphic Art and Drawing,

Zacheta Gallery, Warsaw, 1963
H. Anders, Leszek Rozga, Graphic Art and Drawing,
Zacheta Gallery, Warsaw, 1974
Z. Kucielska and J. Malinowski, Expressionism in Polish
Graphic Art, Muzeum, Narodowe, Krakow, 1976
H. Anders, Leszek Rozga, Graphic Art, Drawing and
Painting, Henning Gallery, Hamburg and BWA Gallery,
Lodz, 1979
W. Wierczowska,Contemporary Polish Drawing, Auriga
Publishers, Warsaw, 1982
D. Wroblewska, Contemporary Polish Graphic Art,
Interpress Publishers, Warsaw, 1983
J. Glowacki, Leszek Rozga, Erotics, 86 Press, Lodz, 1990
S. Stopczyk, H. Anders, D. Wroblewska and M.
Markiewicz, Leszek Rozga, Graphic Art, Drawing,
Watercolours and Gouaches 1982–94, State Gallery,
Lodz, 1995

Krzysztof **Roziewicz**
Individual Exhibitions
1992   Christel Fahrenhost Gallery, Hameln, Germany
        '32' Gallery, Warsaw
Group Exhibitions
1990   Graphic Art from Poland, Frederick Layton
        Gallery, Milwaukee, United States
1991   Museum Academy of Fine Arts, Warsaw
        Gallery GA + MA, Warsaw
        Gallery INTERFABRIK, Nurtinges, Germany
        International Graphic Art Triennale, Sopot
        Graphic Art Biennale, Lodz
1992   The Baltic Countries Graphic Art Triennale,
        Gdansk
        Graphic Art Biennale, Katowice
        Academy of Fine Arts, Warsaw
1993   Academy of Fine Arts, Berlin, Germany
        Graphic Art Biennale, Paris, France
        Museum of History of the Country, Gdansk
1994   The 9th Seoul International Print Biennale,
        Seoul, Korea
        World Award Winners Gallery, Katowice
        International of Graphic Arts, Krakow
1995   The 4th International Print Triennale, Gdansk
1996   Premio Internazionale Biella per l'Incisione,
        Biella, Italy
Prizes
1991   International Mezzotint Triennale, Sopot, Award
1992   Baltic Countries Graphic Art Triennale,
        Gdansk, 2nd Prize
1993   Graphic Art in Warsaw, Award
Works in Collections
National Museum in Gdansk
National Polish Collection of Sacral Art, Warsaw
Gallery 'TEST' Collection, Warsaw
Works in private collections in Poland, Germany,
United States, Sweden, France
Bibliography
R. Peter, 'Art in Poland', Deister Zaitung 27.04.92r.,
Germany
I. Gustowska, Catalogue, 'The Baltic Countries Graphic
Art Triennale', Gdansk, Poland

Tadeusz **Michal Siara**
Selected Individual Exhibitions
1970   Katowice
1973   Lodz, Gydnia
1974   Szczecin, Bialystok
1975   Katowice

Amsterdam, Netherlands
1977 Warsaw
1978 Wroclaw
Stockholm, Sweden
1979 Marburg, Germany
1980 Kristianstad, Sweden
1981 Lublin, Klodzko
1982 Lodz
1983 Opole
Walbrzych
Sofia, Bulgaria
1984 Gliwice
Lilienthal, Germany
Raisio, Kotka, Anjalankoski, Finland
1985 Poznan
1986 Strasbourg, France
1987 Zamosc
1988 Davis, California, United States
1991 Lomza
1993 Katowice
Czestochowa
1994 Neuberg a/d Donau, Germany
1995 Prague, Czech Republic
1996 Giessen, Germany

Selected Group Exhibitions
1974 4th International Graphics Biennale,
Florence, Italy
5th International Graphics Biennale, Krakow
10th International Graphics Biennale,
Menton, France
1976 6th International Graphics Biennale, Krakow
5th International Graphics Biennale,
Bradford, Great Britain
1978 5th International Graphics Biennale, Frechen,
Germany
1979 13th International Graphics Biennale,
Ljubljana, Yugoslavia
1983 7th International Graphics Triennale,
Frechen, Germany
1984 10th International Graphics Biennale, Krakow
World Art Expo, Boston, United States
1985 4th Exhibition of Small Graphic Forms, Lodz
1987 5th Exhibition of Small Graphic Forms, Lodz
1989 6th Exhibition of Small Graphic Forms, Lodz
1990 3rd Triennale of Mini-Graphics, Riga, Latvia
1991 7th Exhibition of Small Graphic Forms, Lodz
(honorary medal)
5th 'Cuprum', Lublin (special award)
1st International Graphics Biennale, Sapporo,
Japan
2nd International Triennale of Small
Graphics, Chamalieres, France
1993 1st International Print Triennale, Maastrict,
Netherlands
13th Mini-Print Internacional, Cadaques,
Spain

Wieslaw **Skibinski**
Individual Exhibitions
1990 Galeria Miejska, Limanowa
1991 Rysunek i grafika, Galeria Podbrzezie, Krakow
1993 Gallery Asteion, Tokyo, Japan
1994 Gallery Asteion, Tokyo, Japan
Group Exhibitions
1985 International Exhibition of Photography,
Kobe, Japan
1988 Grafika mlodych, Galeria Plastyka, Krakow
(nagroda W. Troschke)

1989 Najlepsza grafika Roku, Galeria ASP, Krakow
1990 Najlepsze dyplomy 1988–1989, Torun
Profesorowie i absolwenci ASP w Krakowie,
Netherlands
1991 Nowa sztuka w Palacu, Palac Sztuki (Galeria
Podbrzezie), Krakow
1st Triennale Grafiki Polskiej, BWA Gallery,
Katowice
Micro Art, Galeria ART, Warsaw
1992 Pobyt czasowy (TE7EM), Galeria Miriam,
Tychy
W sierpniu (TE7EM), Galeria Gole Niebo,
Krakow
Neue Kunst aus den alten Krakau, Darmstadt,
Germany
Pieklo-Niebo (TE7EM), Galeria Plastyka,
Krakow
1993 Miedzynarodowy Przeglad Exlibrisu, WBP,
Katowice
TIAS-Targi sztuki, Tokyo, Japan
Grafika w Krakowie–Pokolenia, BWA Gallery,
Krakow
GEO-graphic (TE7EM), Konsulat Austriacki,
Krakow
1994 GEO-graphic (TE7EM), Katowice; Venice,
Italy; Salzburg, Austria
Budapest Art Expo (Stowarzyszenie
Triennale), Budapest, Hungary
Junge Krakauer Graphik, Galerie in Zabo,
Nürnberg, Germany
1st Wystawa srodowiskowa, Galeria Obok,
Tychy
4th zywioly wspolczesnej grafiki polskiej (Jan
Fejkiel Gallery), Krakow Expo Centre, Krakow
Miedzynarodowe Triennale Grafiki, Krakow
Minimal Art, Galeria Kronika, Bytom
Poetes francais, graveurs polonais (Jan Fejkiel
Gallery) Galerie des Franciscains, St Nazaire,
France
1995 Najlepsza Grafika Miesiaca, Galeria Pryzmat,
Krakow
Akcja Fax, Konsulat Austriacki, Krakow
Budapest Art Expo (Jan Fejkiel Gallery),
Budapest, Hungary
Graphik Messe Dresden 1995 (Jan Fejkiel
Gallery), Dresden, Germany

Krzysztof **Skorczewski**
Selected Group Exhibitions
1972 Galeria 33 Milionow, 2 program TVP
Galerie L, Hamburg, Germany
1973 La Galerie des Philosophes, Geneva,
Switzerland
1975 Galeri Pro Arte, Stockholm, Sweden
1980 Galeria 34, Krakow
BWA Gallery, Jelenia Gora
Galeria GP, Warsaw
1981 BWA Gallery, Slupsk
1982 Palazzo Sormani, Milan, Italy
Galeria IL Mercante de Stampe, Milan, Italy
Galerie in Zabo, Nürnberg, Germany
1984 Galeria PN, Warsaw
1985 Centre d'Action Culturelle, Brieuc, France
Galeria Inny Swiat, Krakow
1988 Gallery NDA, Sapporo, Japan
Galeria Inny Swiat, Krakow
Galeria PN, Warsaw
Galeria 72, Poznan

Galeria Joannart, Vicenza, Italy
1991 Muzeum Miedzi, Legnica
Galeria Aneks, Poznan
1992 Galeria Rosso Tiziano Arte, Piacenza, Italy
Galeria PN, Warsaw
Muzeum im. H. Sienkiewicza, Oblegorek
Galerie Inny Swiat i Camelot, Krakow
Polski Instytut Kultury, Prague, Czech
Republic
1993 Instytut Polski, Lipsk
Guilford College Library, Greensboro, United
States
1994 Galeria Balucka, Lodz
Galeria Joannart, Vicenza, Italy
Galeria Brama, Gliwice
Galeria Garbary, Poznan
1995 Carmignano di Breta, Italy
Instytut Kultury Polskiej, Rome, Italy
Galeria Piano Nobile, Krakow
Galerie Provinciale Jan Fejkiel Gallery, Liege,
Belgium

Works in Collections
Muzeum Miedzi, Legnica (pelna kolekcja)
Biblioteka Narodowa, Warsaw
Teatr Studio, Warsaw
Muzeum Narodowe, Warsaw, Krakow, Szczecin, Gdansk
Muzeum im. L. Wyczolkowskiego, Bydgoszcz
Muzeum Ziemi Lubuskiej, Zielona Gora
Albertina Sammlung, Vienna, Austria
Muzeum Sztuki i Historii Fribourg, Switzerland
Museum of Modern Art, New York, United States
University of California, Berkeley, United States
Guilford's Art Gallery, Guilford College, Greensboro,
United States
Harvard University, Divinity School, Cambridge,
United States
And in private collections in Poland and the United
States

Prizes and Awards
1970 Ogolnopolskim Przegladzie Grafiki
Studenckiej w Krakowie, 2nd Nagroda
1971 Konkursie na Najlepsza Grafike Miesiaca w
Krakowie, 1st and 2nd Nagroda
1972 4th Miedzynarodowym Biennale Grafiki w
Krakowie, 3rd Nagroda
1st Wystawie Grafiki Mlodych w Krakowie,
Nagroda Krytyki
Nagroda Towarzystwa Albertina, Vienna
1973 7th Wiosna Opolska, 2nd Nagroda i Medal na
przegladzie
3rd Ogolnopolskim Konkursie Graficznym w
Lodzi, Wyroznienie i Medal
1977 Ogolnopolskim Konkursie Graficznym im.
Jozefa Gielniaka w Jeleniej Gorze, 3rd
Nagroda i Brazowy Medal
1979 4th Krajowej Wystawie Grafiki, Lodz, Nagroda
1986 11th Meidzynarodowym Biennale Grafiki w
Krakowie, Nagroda Fundowana
1989 2nd Festival International de Gravure de
Menton, France, 1st Nagroda
1995 Miedzynarodowym Biennale Grafiki Cuprum
6th w Lubinie, Nagroda specjalna

Jacek **Sroka**
Selected Individual Exhibitions
1985 A. Dzieduszycki & P. Sosnowski Gallery,
Warsaw
1986 L. K. Gallery, Varrelbusch, Germany

1987　M. Gologorski and D. Rostworowski Gallery,
Krakow
Langbrok Gallery, Reykjavik, Iceland
Teatre STU Gallery, Krakow
1988　Iona Stichting Gallery, Amsterdam,
Netherlands
W. Asperger Gallery, Knittligen, Germany
1989　Signe Gallery, Heerlen, Netherlands
1991　'Berliner Bilder', W. Asperger Studio Gallery,
Berlin, Germany
1992　'Death by Water', The Historical Musem of
Krakow, The Town Hall Tower, Krakow
'Building the World', Jan Fejkiel Gallery, Krakow
1994　Post & Salamon Contemporary Art,
Brunssum, Netherlands
1995　State Art Gallery, Lodz
Galerie Marianne Grob, Lucerne, Switzerland
Galerie MMG, Tokyo, Japan
Les Cascades (Galerie Denis Canteux), Paris,
France

Selected Group Exhibitions

1984　'Welt & Krakau', Museum Fridericianum,
Kassel, Germany
De La Marmita Gallery, Cordoba, Spain
1985　4 Europaische Grafik-Biennale Baden
Baden, Baden Baden, Germany
'Printed in Krakow', World Print Council, San
Francisco, United States
3rd International Triennale der Zeichnung,
Nürnberg, Germany
16th International Print Biennale Exhibition,
Ljubljana, Yugoslavia
1986　Galerie Bernanos, Paris, France
'Polish Prints — Prints from the Graphic Arts
Faculty of the Academy of Fine Arts', Krakow;
Atrium Gallery, University of Connecticut,
Storrs, United States
First Annual International Miniature Art
Exhibition, Del Bello Gallery, Toronto,
Canada
'Consument Art '86', Kunstmarkt Nürnberg,
Germany
1987　4th Mostra Internazionale di Grafika, Catania,
Italy
'Grafica Atlantica', Kjarvalsstadir Museum,
Reykjavik, Iceland
4th Print Triennale Exhibition, Vaasa, Finland
'Krakauer Grafiken der Gegenwart',
Volkshochschule, Bad Oeynhausen, Germany
1988　'5 x 30', BWA Gallery, Bialystok
'Wet Paint', Zacheta, Warsaw
'Gravure polonaise contemporaine', Club 44,
La Chaux de Fonds, Switzerland
'Le Cadavre Repris', BWA Gallery, Krakow
6th Print Biennale Exhibition, Seoul, Korea
'Master Prints from Poland', Santa Fe
Community College, Sante Fe, United States
1989　'Gravures de l'Academie des Beaux Arts de
Cracovie', Hotel de Ville de Chatelet, Belgium
'Young Polish Painting 1982-87', National
Painting Gallery, Lvov, Ukraine
Artistic Studios Gallery, Moscow, Russia
'Polish Prints, A Contemporary Graphic
Tradition', University of Nebraska, Lincoln,
United States
1990　'New Art in the Palace', Palac Sztuki TPSP,
Krakow
'Bissige Hunde', Galerie Signe, Aachen,
Germany

'Freedom, 100 Drawings from Within',
Commons Gallery, University of Hawaii,
Manoa, United States
'The Expressive Struggle, Twenty-Six
Contemporary Polish Artists', The New
Academy of Art, New York, United States
1991　'Positionen Polen', Kunstlerhaus Bethanien,
Berlin, Germany
'The Struggle for Self Image', Boston Centre
for the Arts, Boston, United States
Art Fair 'Lineart', Post & Salamon
Contemporary Art, Gent, Belgium
1992　'The Expressive Struggle, Twenty-Six
Contemporary Polish Artists', Anderson
Gallery, Buffalo, United States
'Four Polish Painters', Asperger Gallery,
Strasbourg, France
'Impressions Polonaises', Arthoteque, Musee
Savoisien, Chambery, France
'Jetzt — Teraz', Polnische Gratik der
Gegenwart, Creditanstalt, Vienna, Austria
1993　'Polnische Graphic in der Albertina',
Albertina, Vienna, Austria
'Ironical Portrait', BWA Gallery, Krakow
Art Fair 'Saga', Galerie Denis Canteux, Paris,
France
'Artists from Krakow', Zacheta Gallery, Warsaw
Art Fair 'Art Multiple', Dusseldorf, Post &
Salamon Contemporary Art, Dusseldorf,
Germany
Art Fair, 'Lineart', Post & Salamon
Contemporary Art, Gent, Belgium
1994　Art Fair 'Art Cologne', Eva Poll Gallery,
Cologne, Germany
'Pantera', Post & Salamon Contemporary Art,
Brunssun, Netherlands
'Teraz —Now' (Polish Award Winners of
International Print Exhibitions), Broome
Street Gallery, New York, United States
'Widerstand und Aufbruch', Polnische Kunst
1980–93, Stadt Stuttgart Rathaus, Stuttgart,
Germany
1995　Art Fair 'Saga', Galerie Denis Canteux, Paris,
France
15th Stockholm Art Fair, Post & Salamon
Contemporary Art, Stockholm, Sweden
Art Fair 'Art Multiple', Post & Salamon
Contemporary Art, Dusseldorf, Germany

Prizes and Awards

1981　Polish Ministry of Culture Prize for Diploma
Work
1984　6th European Biennale of Graphic Art,
Mulhouse, France, Prize
1986　Young Graphic Art Review, Plastyka Gallery,
Krakow, Prize
1st International Miniature Exhibition, Del
Bello Gallery, Toronto, Canada, Mention
1987　Graphica Atlantica, Reykjavik, Iceland, 3rd
Prize
4th International Graphic Biennale, Vaasa,
Finland, Grand Prix
National Print Competition, Lodz, Mention
1988　St Wyspianski National Prize for Young Artist
6th International Graphic Biennale, Seoul,
Korea, Grand Prix
5th Quadriennale of Small Graphics,
Bratislava, Czechoslovakia, Mention
1991　Best Print of the Month Competition, Krakow,
Grand Prix

1994　International Graphic Triennale, Krakow,
Trybowski Prize
1995　Cuprum Competition, Lubin, Mention
1996　Best Print of the Month Competition, Krakow,
Mention

Works in Collections

National Museum, Krakow
Regional Museum, Bydgoszcz
Historical Museum of the City of Krakow
Print Collection, Polish Academy of Science, Krakow
Museum Fridericianum, Kassel, Germany
British Museum, London, Great Britain
Bibliotheque Nationale, Paris, France
Musee Savoisien, Chambery, France
Metropolitan Museum of Modern Art, New York,
United States
Graphische Sammlung, Albertina, Vienna, Austria
Museum Prefectoral, Kumamoto, Japan
Print Kabinett, Leyden, Netherlands
Kjarvalsstadir Museum, Reykjavik, Iceland
Sprovieri Collection, Paris, France
Asperger Collection, Knittlingen, Germany
Also public collections in Egypt, Slovakia, Brazil, South
Korea and Germany

Marcin **Surzycki**

Individual Exhibitions

1990　Galeria ASP, Krakow
1995　Zutphen, Netherlands

Selected Group Exhibitions

1989　'Gravures de l'Academie des Beaux Arts de
Cracovie', Chatelet, Belgium
'Fama '89', Festiwal artystyczny, Szczecin
6th Exposition d'Art Contemporian Polonaise,
Saillans, France
15th International Independent Exhibition of
Prints, Kanagawa, Japan
1990　1st International Triennale Exhibition of
Print, Kochi-Ken, Japan
International Fine Art Exhibition, 3rd Art of
Today', Budapest, Hungary
'Najmlodsi Graficy Krakowa', BWA Gallery,
Krakow
'Junge Grafik aus Krakau', Leipzig, Germany
9th International Exhibition of Graphic Art,
Frechen, Germany
3rd Ogolnopolskie Biennale Grafiki, 'Wobec
Wartosci', Katowice
5th Busan Biennale International Art
Exhibition', Busan, Korea
1991　International Triennale of Graphic Arts,
Krakow
Triennale Grafiki Polskiej, BWA Gallery,
Katowice
Ogolnopolska wystawa grafiki, 'Kolor w
Grafice', BWA Gallery, Torun
'Grafika Polska', Maastricht, Netherlands
'Face to Face', Contemporary Printmaking
from Poland and United States, Fine Arts
Gallery, Gainsville, Florida, United States
International Print Exhibition, 'Intergrafia',
Katowice
Consumenta '91, 'Nachbarn', Nürnberg,
Germany
The International Prints Exhibition, 'Eastern
Europe – Japan', Kanagawa, Japan
'Jan Fejkiel Gallery Collection', Stockholm,
Sweden

12 Ogolnopolska Pokonkursowa Wystawa Grafiki, BWA Gallery, Lodz
Art Polonais, Galerie Ewa, Toulon, France
Kunst in Europa 1992, Bad Kissingen, Germany

1992 Polnische Graphik, Galeria in Zabo, Nürnberg, Germany
'Wystawa Piaciu', Kulturcentrum, Ronneby, Sweden
Exhibition of Polish Prints, Retretti, Finland
Art Contemporain Polonais, Toulon, France
Neue Kunst aus Krakau, Darmstad, Germany

1993 'Portret Ironiczny. Groteska we wspolczesnej grafice krakowskiej', BWA & Jan Fejkiel Gallery, Krakow
'Award Winners Gallery', Augsburg, Germany
10th International Exhibition of Graphic Art, Frechen, Germany
20th International Biennale of Graphic Art, Ljubljana, Slovenia
Orginal-Graphik internationaler Preistrager aus Krakau, 'Segment 3', Nürnberg, Germany
1st International Biennale of Graphic Art Exhibition, Maastricht, Netherlands
The 12th International Exchange Exhibition of Prints, Seoul, Korea
'Piekny prezent', Galeria Sztuki A. B. Wahl, Warsaw

1994 2nd Triennale Grafiki Polskiej, BWA Gallery, Katowice
Laureci Grand Prix Ogolnopolskiego Biennale Grafiki, 'Wobec wartosci', Katowice
Wystawa Wydzialu Grafiki ASP Krakow; Wimbledon Croydon, Great Britain
4th International Art Fair Art Expo, Budapest, Hungary
International Print Triennale, Krakow
'Intergrafia', World Award Winners Gallery, Katowice
5th International Triennale 1994 Print, Contemporary Art Competition, Osaka, Japan
Polish Award Winners of International Print Exhibition, 'Teraz-Now', Broome Street Gallery, New York, United States
1st International Triennale of Graphic Art, Bitola, Macedonia
Print Exhibition, 'Krakow', Pecs, Hungary

1995 Laureaci konkursow, 'Najlepsza Grafika Miesiaca 1991-94', Krakow
21st International Biennale of Graphic Art, Ljubljana, Slovenia
'Grafika krakowska, Jan Fejkiel Gallery', Panstwowa Galeria Sztuki Wspolczesnej, Przemysl
Jan Fejkiel Gallery, Targi Sztuki, Budapest, Hungary; Dresden, Germany
'Nowa Grafika Polska', Galeria Prowincjonalna, Slubice
'Neue Graphik aus Polen', Galerie Gallus, Frankfurt, Germany

Prizes and Awards
1990 Wystawa najlepszych prac dyplomowych wyzszych uczelni plastycznych', Torun, Prize
9th International Exhibition of Graphic Art', Frechen, Germany, Prize
3 Ogolnopolskie Biennale Grafiki, 'Wobec wartosci', Katowice, Grand Prix
1991 International Print Exhibition, 'Intergrafia', Katowice, Prize

1995 Najlepsza Grafika Miesiaca, ZPAP, Krakow, Grand Prix

Works in Collections
Museum Albertina, Vienna, Austria
Muzeum Okregowe, Bydgoszcz
Muzeum Archidiecezjaine, Katowice
Private collections in Poland and abroad

Jacek **Szewczyk**
Selected Group Exhibitions
1985 International Exlibris Competition, Sint Niklaas, Belgium
1986 1st Triennale of Drawing, Kalisz-86
1987 Small Graphic Forms Exhibition, Lodz
1st Annual Drawing Competition, Lublin
6th Woodcut and Linocut Competition, Jelenia Gora
1990 The Academy of Fine Arts and Design 1946-90, Students and Teachers Exhibition, CBW Zacheta, Warsaw
1991 Sudwestlb Printed Graphic Art Prize, Stuttgart, Germany
10th Cleveland International Drawing Biennale, Cleveland, Great Britain
5th International Drawing Triennale, Wroclaw
1992 Polish Culture Institute in Stockholm, Drawing and Print Exhibition, Stockholm, Sweden
2nd Biennale Internacional de Grabado, Orense, Spain
'10 years later 1982-92', Exhibition of Contemporary Polish Drawing, Radom, Krakow
Grand Prix Faber-Castell Drawing Competition, Poznan
1993 Exhibition of Prints, 'Stockholm in Wroclaw', Museum Academy of Fine Art and Design, Wroclaw
Sudwestlb Printed Graphic Art Prize, Stuttgart, Germany
11th Cleveland International Drawing Biennale, Cleveland, Great Britain
10th Internationale Grafik Triennale, Frechen, Germany
1st Internationale Grafiek Biennale, Maastricht, Netherlands
2nd International Biennale of Graphic Arts, Gyor, Hungary
1994 'Polish and Swedish Prints Exhibition', The Baltic Sea Culture Centre, Gdansk
13th Polish Open Print Competition, Lodz
2nd Triennale of Polish Print, Katowice
Graphik Messe Gallery, 'Na Odwachu', Dresden, Germany
Gallery 'Na Solnym', Drawing Exhibition', 'Fabryczna', Wroclaw
3rd Bienal Internacional de Grabado, Orense, Spain
Grafiska Sallskapets Galleri, Orjan Wikstrom/Jacek Szewczyk Print Exhibition, Stockholm, Sweden
Gallery 'Na Odwachu', Selected Polish Graphic Artist in Wroclaw, Wroclaw
Seoul International Print Biennale, Seoul, Korea
Academy of Fine Art and Design, Wroclaw in Brunswick, Germany
1995 Konstframjandet, Mikael Kihlman/Jacek

Szewczyk Print and Drawing Exhibition, Orebro, Sweden
11th Norsk Internasjonal Grafik Triennale, Fredrikstad, Norway
Graphik Messe, Gallery 'Na Odwachu', Dresden, Germany
Young Printmakers from Wroclaw, Print exhibition, Gallery 'Na Odwachu', Wroclaw and Gallery 'Garbary 48', Poznan
Pawlikowska, Tryszkiewicz, Szewczyk, Nowicki, Print and Drawing exhibition, Gallery 'Na Wzgorzu', Lubin
1996 Gallery 'Bacchus', Mikael Kihlman and Jacek Szewczyk, Print and Drawing Exhibition, Boras, Sweden
Graphik Messe, Gallery 'Na Odwachu', Dresden, Germany
Akademie der Kunste, Berlin and Gunter Grass Foundation of Daniel Chodowiecki, Drawing Competition, Berlin, Germany; Sopot, Poland

Awards
1986 1st Triennale of Drawing, Kalisz-86, Regular Award
1987 1st Annual Drawing Competition, Lublin, 1st Prize
6th Woodcut and Linocut Competition, Jelenia Gora, Special Award for Young Artists and Regular Award
1990 18th Polish Museums Poster Review, Przemysl, 2nd Prize
1991 Sudwestlb Printed Graphic Art Prize, Stuttgart, Germany, 3rd Prize
1993 11th Cleveland International Drawing Biennale, Cleveland, Great Britain, 2nd Prize
1994 3rd Bienal Internacional de Grabado, Orense, Spain, Gold Medal and 1st Prize
1995 11th Norsk Internasjonal Grafik Triennale, Fredrikstad, Norway, Jury Award

Works in Collections
National Library, Warsaw
Ossolinskich Library, Wroclaw
Cabinet of Prints, Polish Academy of Sciences, Krakow
Museum of Contemporary Art, Boras, Sweden

Barbara **Szubinska**
Selected Individual Exhibitions
1958 Klub Studencki 'Hybrydy', Warsaw
1963 Salon Debiutow, Warsaw
1966 Galeria Sztuki Wspolczesnej, Warsaw
1967 Foyer Teatru STS, Warsaw
1971 Galerie l'Angle Aigu, Brussels, Belgium
BWA Gallery, Bialystok, Lublin
1972 Galeria l'Angle Aigu, Brussels, Belgium
Galeria MDM, Warsaw
1973 Galerie Liebelt, Marburg, Germany
BWA Gallery, Rzeszow, Zielona Gora
1976 Dom Artysty Plastyka, Warsaw
Galeria Srodowisk Tworczych, Olsztyn
1978 Galerie Ingeleiv, Bergen, Norway
1979 Centrum Artystyczne Srodowisk Tworczych, Rome, Italy
1980 Galeria 82, Chelm
Le Centre Artistique, Versoix, Switzerland
1981 Galerie Klosa, Varrelbush, Germany
1982 Galeria 'Sztuka Polska', Berlin Zachodni, Berlin, Germany
1983 Galerie Ingeleiv, Bergen, Norway

1984	BWA Gallery, Rzeszow		'Skojarzenia', Galeria Malarstwa
1985	Galerie du Chateau, Avenches, Switzerland		Wspolczesnego, Warsaw
1986	Baszta Czarownic, Slupsk		Wystawa 26 Malarzy Polskich, Malmo, Sweden
	Galerie du Bourg, Fribourg, Switzerland		Wystawa Malarzy Warszawskich, Aarhus,
	Galerie Hergeroder, Bielefeld, Germany		Denmark
1987	Galeria 'et', Versmold, Germany	1970	Wystawa 6 malarzy warszawskich, Dwor Artusa,
	Versmolder Kunstkres e. v., Versmold,		Gdansk
	Germany		3rd Festiwal Sztuk Pieknych, Zacheta, Warsaw
1988	Galeria Sztuki Alicji i Bozeny Wahl, Warsaw	1971	Wystawa malarstwa 'Obraz do M-3', Galeria
	'Encyclopaedia Zoologica', Galeria Test,		MDM, Warsaw
	Warsaw		5th Wystawa Plastyki 'Zlotego grona', Zielona
1989	BWA Gallery, Nowy Sacz		Gora
	Osrodki Polskiej Kultury i Informacji, Prague,		'Ars aquae' — Ogolnopolska wystawa akwareli
	Lipsk, Czechoslovakia		i gwaszy, BWA Gallery, Katowice, Poznan
1990	Galeria Salustowicz, Bielefeld, Germany	1972	Poulaisia Kuvia Polska Bilder, Helsinki,
1991	BWA Gallery, Bydgoszcz, Walbrzych		Finland
	Muzeum Okregowe, Walbrzych	1973	'Ars aquae' — Ogolnopolska wystawa akwareli
	Gipssammlung Antriker Skulptur, Berlin,		i gwaszy, BWA Gallery, Katowice, Poznan
	Germany		Spotkania krakowskie — Nasz czas, Artysta
1993	Galeria Agnieszki Bielinskiej, Brussels,		wobec cywilizacji, BWA Gallery, Krakow
	Belgium		Wystawa Rysunku Okregu Warszawskiego
	BWA Gallery, Zamosc		ZPAP, Zacheta, Warsaw
1995	Galeria Milano, Warsaw		Czlowiek XX wieku, Galeria ZPAP, Warsaw
	Galeria Zapiecek, Warsaw		Stadtische Kunsthalle, Mannheim, Germany
1996	Muzeum Sztuki Wspolczesnej, Radom		Wystawa Malarstwa, Baltimore, United States
	Galeria Test, Warsaw		Wystawa Malarstwa, Stockholm, Sweden

Selected Group Exhibitions

1958	14th Ogolnopolska Wystawa Plastyki, Muzeum		Wystawa Malarstwa Polskiego, Yokohama,
	Miejskie, Radom		Japan; Budapest, Hungary
1961	Polskie Dzielo Plastyczne na XV-lecie PRL,	1974	5th Festiwal Sztuk Pieknych, Zacheta, Warsaw
	Muzeum Narodowe, Warsaw		'Ogolnopolski plener malarski — Kazimierz
	17th Ogolnopolska Wystawa Plastyki, Radom		n/Wisla', wystawa poplenerowa, BWA Gallery,
1962	Wystawa malarstwa, rzezby i grafiki 'Otwarte		Lublin
	drzwi', Pomaranczarnia, Warsaw		Salon Letni, Galeria MDM, Warsaw
	9th Wystawa Malarstwa i Grafiki Okregu		Galeria 20, Hanover, Germany
	Warszawskiego ZPAP, Zacheta, Warsaw		Wystawa Malarstwa Polskiego, Bucharest,
1963	4th Ogolnopolska Wystawa Mlodego		Romania
	Malarstwa, Rzezby i Grafiki, BWA Gallery,	1975	Romantyzm i romantycznosc w sztuc polskiej
	Sopot		XIX i XX wieku, Zacheta, Warsaw
1964	Wystawa Mlodych Plastykow Warszawskich	1976	6th Festiwal Sztuk Pieknych, Zacheta, Warsaw
	Grupy 'Rekonesans', Galeria MDM, Warsaw		8th Festiwal Polskiego Malarstwa
	Wystawa gwaszy i rysunkow, Teatr STS, Warsaw		Wspolczesnego, Zamek Ksiazat Pomorskich,
	10th Wystawa Malarstwa Okregu		Szczecin
	Warszawskiego ZPAP, Zacheta, Warsaw		'Autoportret', Salon Sztuki Wspolczesnej
	19th Ogolnopolska Wystawa Plastyki, Radom		'ART', Warsaw
1965	'20th lat PRL w tworczosci plastycznej',		4 Artisti di Varsovia, Milan, Italy
	Zacheta, Warsaw	1977	Wystawa malarstwa grupy warszawskiej, BWA
	Ogolnopolska Wystawa Mlodego Malarstwa,		Gallery, Opole
	BWA Gallery, Sopot		Dom Artysty Plastyka, Warsaw
1966	Mloda Generacja 1960–66, BWA Gallery, Sopot		Polnische Kűnst, Stadtische Kunsthalle,
	3rd Wystawa warszawskich malarzy i rzezbiarzy		Rothenburg, Germany; Stadtische
	Grupy 'Rekonesans', Galeria MDM, Warsaw		Kunsthalle, Darmstadt, Germany
1967	5th Biennale Mlodych, Paris, France	1979	23rd Festiwal Sztuk Plastycznych 'Porownania
	Wystawa Malarstwa Polskiego, Osrodki Kultury		— logika — zmysly', BWA Gallery Sopot
	i Informacji Polskiej Berlin, Germany;		3rd Triennale Malarstwa i Grafiki, Lodz
	Bratislava, Czechoslovakia; Budapest,	1981	35th Ogolnopolski Salon Zimowy Plastyki,
	Hungary; Prague, Czechoslovakia; Sofia,		TPSP, Radom
	Bulgaria		Wystawy malarstwa, grafiki i tkaniny Ruchu
	Wystawa Malarzy Warszawskich, Richard		Artystycznego 'Swiat', Warsaw
	Demarco Gallery, London, Edinburgh,	1984	Wystawy malarstwa, grafiki i tkaniny
	Oxford, Great Britain		Artystycznego 'Swiat', Warsaw
	Memorial Nadiezdy Petrovic, Cacak,		Galeria Sztuki Polskiej, Chojnice
	Yugoslavia	1985	Wystawa Malarstwa i Grafiki Artystow
1968	2nd Festiwal Sztuk Pieknych, Zacheta, Warsaw		Srodowiska Warszawskiego, Zacheta, Warsaw
	4th Festiwal Malarstwa Wspolczesnego,	1986	Wystawy malarstwa, grafiki i tkaniny Ruchu
	Szczecin		Artystycznego 'Swiat', Warsaw
	2nd Triennale Rysunku, Wroclaw		'Artysci Warszawy dla Warszawy', Dom Wojska
1969	4th Wystawa Plastyki 'Zlotego Grona', Zielona		Polskiego, Warsaw
	Gora		'Zycie ludzkie — los ziemi', Zacheta, Warsaw
		1987	Wystawy malarstwa, grafiki i tkaniny Ruchu

	Artystycznego 'Swiat', Warsaw
	4th Targi Sztuki Krajow Socjalistycznych
	'Interart '87', Poznan
	'Inspiracje plockie', BWA Gallery, Plock
	'Studium czerwieni', Galeria Brama, Warsaw
	Sztuka Polska, Algiers, Algeria
1988	Wystawy malarstwa, grafiki i tkaniny Ruchu
	Artystycznego 'Swiat', Warsaw
	4th Miedzynarodowe Triennale Rysunku,
	Wroclaw
1989	Otwarte drzwi, Kopenhaga, Charlottenburg,
	Denmark
	Galeria Espace-Temps, Paris, France
	Generacje, Dni Warszawy, Prague,
	Czechoslovakia
1992	'Szkice do autoportretu', Muzeum Sztuki
	Wspolczesnej, Radom
	'10 lat pozniej', Wystawa rysunku
	wspolczesnego, Muzeum Okregowe, Radom,
	BWA Gallery, Krakow, Lodz
	5th Miedzynarodowe Triennale Rysunku,
	Wroclaw
1994	'Ars erotica', Muzeum Narodowe, Warsaw
	Wystawa Grupy 'Rekonesans', Zacheta,
	Warszawa, BWA Gallery Bydgoszcz
	Wystawa 'EAS przedstawia', Olsztyn,
	BWA Gallery, Plock
1995	Ogolnopolskie Impresje Mikolowskie,
	Muzeum Slaskie, Katowice

Bogdan **Topor**
Individual Exhibition

1991	BWA Gallery, Katowice (Drawings and
	Graphics)

Group Exhibitions

1986	'Print with a Point', Bristol, United Kingdom
	'Wobec wartosci', Muzeum Diecezjalne,
	Katowice
1987	'Dyplom '87', Zacheta Gallery, Warsaw
	'Wspolnota', Muzeum Diecezjalne, Katowice
	Annual Exhibition of Miniature Art, Toronto,
	Canada
1988	'Arsenal '88', Warsaw
	6th International Print Biennale, Seoul, Korea
	12th International Print Biennale, Krakow
1989	'Male Formy w Grafice', Lodz
	'L'Europe des graveurs', Grenoble, France
1990	9th International Graphic Triennale, Frechen,
	Germany
	Annual Exhibition of Miniature Art, Toronto,
	Canada
	5th International Triennale of Graphic Art,
	Vaasa, Finland
1991	12th Ogolnopolska Wystawa Grafiki, Lodz
	1st Triennale Grafiki Polskiej, Katowice
	(Distinction)
1992	4th Ogolnopolska Biennale, Katowice
	(Distinction)
	5th International Drawing Triennale, Wroclaw
1993	1st International Graphic Triennale,
	Maastrict, Netherlands
	2nd International Graphic Biennale, Sapporo,
	Japan
	1st Polish Drawing Triennale, Lubachow
	(Grand Prix)

Jacek **Waltos**

Selected Individual Exhibitions

1990 'Dr Freud …', Horn Gallery, Poznan
1991 'Dr Freud …', Kordegarda Gallery, Warsaw
1993 'Eleven Pictures', City of Krakow Museum of History, Town Hall Tower, Krakow
1996 'Between Painting and Sculpture', Retrospective Individual Exhibition 1961–92, Galeria 'Arsenal', Poznan; Centre of Polish Sculpture, Oronsko; BWA Gallery, Katowice

Selected Group Exhibitions

1990 'Aus der Metapher Heraus' (From the metaphor and back), Darmstadt, Germany
1991 'Dotyk/Touch: Iconography of the Eighties', BWA Gallery, Palace of Art, Krakow
1992 'Ten Years Later', drawing exhibition, Contemporary Art Museum, Radom
The Polish National Fund, auction of contemporary Polish paintings, New York, United States
1993 'To Show the Invisible', Jesuit's Gallery, Poznan
'The Krakow Spleen', The Union of Polish Artists Gallery, Warsaw
1994 'Ars Erotica', Pro Arte Foundation & National Museum, Warsaw
'The Bible in Contemporary Artists' Intuition', National Museum, Gdansk
'44 Artists against Jan Matejko', National Museum, Krakow
'Della Passione' (On the Passion), Polish Institute of Culture, Rome, Italy

Witold **Warzywoda**

Participated in more than 100 group exhibitions and competitions between 1979 and 1995 as well as presenting his own creation at 21 individual shows in Poland and abroad.

Works in Collections

Museum of the History of the City of Lodz, Lodz
Museum of the Warsaw Archdiocese, Warsaw
National Library, Warsaw
University Library, Lodz
Jozef Pilsudski Library, Lodz
Central Bureau of Art Exhibitions, Warsaw
State Art Galleries in Lodz, Torun, Radom, Piotrkow Trybunalski, Biala Podlaska
Cul-des-Arts, Couvin, Belgium
ExLibris Museum, Malbork
Numerous private collections in Poland and abroad

Tadeusz **Gustaw Wiktor**

Individual Exhibitions

1973 'Poeza Symbolu, Poeza Swiatpogladu', ASP Gallery, Krakow
1975 'Paintings', Penderecki Symposium, Krakow
'Paintings', Florianska Gallery, Krakow
'Paintings', KMPiK Gallery, Krakow
1976 'Grafika Niemultiplikacyja', B Gallery, Krakow
1977 'Metryka Zespolu', Gallery 2, Krakow
1978 'Zbioru 25', 3rd Music Festival, Baranow, Zamek
1981 'Transrealizm', Maly Rynek Gallery, Krakow
1982 'Graphics and Paintings', GTO-ASP Gallery, Krakow
1983 'T. G. Wiktor, Graphics and Drawings', Norrköpings Konstmuseum, Norway

1984 'Transrealizm', Black Gallery, Krakow
1986 'Wiktor', Prix ex aequo award exhibition at 10th Krakow International Print Biennale, Pryzmat Gallery, Krakow
1987 'Dialog z Malewiczem', University Gallery of Contemporary Art, Cieszyn
1989 'Znikad Nigdzie Donikad', Krzysztofory Gallery, Krakow
'Wiktor', Florianska Gallery, Krakow
'Wiktor, Studio BP', BWA Gallery, Sandomierz
'Wiktor', Gallery '72, Chelm
1990 'Wiktor', Grand Prix award exhibition at 11th International Original Drawing Exhibition, Museum of Contemporary Art, Contemporary Art Gallery, Rijeka
'Wiktor, Studio BP', Gallery of Contemporary Art, Zamosc
1992 'Drawings, Paintings', Aula-ASP Gallery, Warsaw
1993 'Drawings and Paintings', BWA Gallery, Lodz
1994 'Drawings and Paintings', BWA Gallery, Slupsk, Bielsko-Biala, Opole
1996 'Paintings', Artemis Gallery, Krakow

Group Exhibitions

1978 International Print Biennale, Krakow
International Drawing Triennale, Wroclaw
'Intergrafia' Katowice
1979 International Graphic Biennale, Ljubljana, Yugoslavia
1980 Norwegian International Graphic Biennale, Fredrikstad, Norway
International Impact Art Festival, Kyoto, Japan
International Print Biennale, Krakow
1981 2nd European Graphic Biennale, Baden Baden, Germany
International Drawing Triennale, Wroclaw
International Graphic Biennale, Ljubljana, Yugoslavia
International Impact Art Festival, Kyoto, Japan
1982 7th International Print Biennale, Bradford, Great Britain
International Exhibition of Original Drawings, Rijeka, Yugoslavia
International Mail-Art Exhibition, Seoul, Korea
2nd Convergence of Young Expression, Paris, France
International Impact Art Festival, Kyoto, Japan
1983 International Seminar of Experimental Art, Norrköping, Norway
9th Independent Exhibition of Print, Kanagawa, Japan
International Impact Art Festival, Kyoto, Japan
International Graphic Biennale, Ljubljana, Yugoslavia
1984 Premio Internazionale Biella per l'Incisione, Beilla, Italy
International Engraving Biennale, Gerpinnes, Belgium
International Print Exhibition, Kassel, Germany
International Print Biennale, Krakow
Prizewinners of the Krakow International Print Biennale 1966–80, Krakow
International Impact Art Festival, Kyoto, Japan
International Mail-Art Exhibition, Budapest, Hungary
'Intergrafia', Katowice

1985 International Experimental Art Exhibition, Budapest, Hungary
International Graphic Biennale, Ljubljana, Yugoslavia
1986 'Consument ART', Nürnberg, Germany
International Print Biennale, Krakow
'Intergrafia', Katowice
1987 'Geometria i lad', Chelm
International Graphic Biennale, Ljubljana, Yugoslavia
1988 3rd Annual Exhibition of Miniature Art, Toronto, Canada
'Interart '88', Poznan
International Exhibition of Original Drawings, Rijeka, Yugoslavia
'De stand van zaken', Maastrict, Netherlands
International Print Biennale, Krakow
'Intergrafia', Katowice
1989 'Geometry, Science and Mysticism', Chelm
'RIPOPEE 2', La Louviere, Belgium
'The Countries of the East', International Print Festival, Menton, France
1990 International Impact Art Festival, Kyoto, Japan
1991 'Consument ART', Nürnberg, Germany
'Geometria i Swiatlo', Chelm
'From Milan to Krakow — 100 Books from the Vanni Scheiwiller Collection', Krakow
'Intergrafia', La Louviere, Belgium
'Intergrafia', Katowice
International Graphic Biennale, Ljubljana, Slovenia
1992 5th International Drawing Triennale, Wroclaw
'Construction and Sign', Wlodawa
'Consument ART '92', Nürnberg, Germany
'Intergrafia '91 — Art Fair', Augsburg, Germany
International Drawing Triennale, Wroclaw
1993 'Spojrzenie wstecz', Katowice
'Winners' Gallery', Augsburg, Germany
'Vanni Scheiwiller book editions', Lodz
'From the Chelm Collection', Warsaw
'Construction and Sign', Chelm
'SIAC Congress', Krakow
'Form and Thought', Chelm
1994 International Art Exhibition, Budapest, Hungary
International Print Triennale, Krakow

Awards

1978 7th International Print Triennale, Krakow, Special Prize
1983 Polish Cultural Foundation, Norrköping, Norway, Scholarship
1984 10th International Print Biennale, Krakow, Prix ex aequo
1986 11th International Print Biennale, Krakow, 'Project' Prize
1988 11th International Exhibition of Original Drawings, Rijeka, Grand Prix
and 12 major Polish awards

Works in Collections

Panstwowa Galeria Sztuki, Lodz
Muzeum Okregowe im. L. Wyczolkowskiego, Bydgoszcz
Muzeum Regionalne, Chojnice
Muzeum Slaskie, Katowice
Muzeum Okregowe, Konin
Biblioteka WSP, Zielona Gora
Muzeum Narodowe, Gdansk
Muzeum Okregowe, Koszalin
Stowarzyszenie Miedzynarodowe Triennale Grafiki, Krakow

Muzeum Okregowe, Chelm
Biblioteka Narodowa, Warsaw
Muzeum Narodowe, Szczecin
Norrköping Konstmuseum, Norrköping, Norway
Centre de la Gravure et de l'Image Imprimee, La
Louviere, Belgium
International Art Centre, Kyoto, Japan
Club of Young Artists, Budapest, Hungary
Portland Art Museum, Portland, Oregon, United States
Del Bello Gallery, Toronto, Canada
Vanni Scheiwiller and A. Kalczynska Collection, Milan,
Italy
Museum of Modern Art, Rijeka, Yugoslavia
Slovakian National Museum, Bratislava, Slovakia
Musée du Petit Format, Cul-des-Sarts, Couvin, Belgium

Ewa **Zawadzka**

Individual Exhibitions

1984	ON Gallery, Poznan
	Black Gallery, Krakow
1988	DESA Gallery, Krakow
1989	BWA Gallery, Lodz
	BWA Gallery, Katowice
	Gallery 72, Poznan
	Hoza 40 Gallery, Warsaw
1990	BWA Gallery, Czestochowa
1992	F15 Gallery, Moss, Norway
	Brama Gallery, Gliwice
1993	Mala Grafiki Gallery, Lublin
	Extravagance Miejska Gallery, Sosnowiec
	MADA Gallery, Karlsruhe, Germany
	XYLON Museum, Schetzingen, Germany
1994	Kronika Art Centre, Bytom
	BWA Gallery, Zielona Gora
1995	Artemis Gallery, Krakow

Group Exhibitions

1986	International Print Biennale, Krakow
	International Graphics Biennale, Gerpinnes, Belgium
	Premio Internazionale Biella per l'Incisione, Biella, Italy
1988	International Print Biennale, Krakow
1989	Young Drawing Triennale, Nürnberg, Germany
1990	International Art Festival, Kyoto, Japan
	European Graphics, Art Museum of Grenoble, France
	International Art Festival, Valparaiso, Chile
	Intergrafic '90, Berlin, Germany
	Art Fair, Chicago, United States
	Art Fair, Cologne, Germany
1991	Art Fair, Frankfurt, Germany
	Art Fair, Cologne, Germany
	Art Fair, Frankfurt, Germany
	Art Fair, Chicago, United States
1992	Art Fair, Tokyo, Japan
	Art Fair, Frankfurt, Germany
	International Graphics Triennale, Fredrikstad, Norway
	International Graphics Triennale, Kochi, Japan
	Art Fair, Cologne, Germany
1993	Art Fair, Frankfurt, Germany
	Art Fair, Cologne, Germany
	International Graphics Triennale, Giza, Egypt
1994	Art Fair, Frankfurt, Germany
	Art Fair, Cologne, Germany
	Recommended for Augsburg, prizewinners' exhibition, Augsburg, Germany
	Polish Graphics Triennale, Katowice
	International Print Triennale, Krakow
	Intergrafia '94, Katowice
	International Graphics Triennale, Osaka, Japan
1995	Art Fair, Frankfurt, Germany

Awards

1986	International Print Biennale, Krakow, Prix ex aequo
1988	International Print Biennale, Krakow, Medal of Honour
1989	Young Drawing Triennale, Nürnberg, Germany, Prize
1992	International Graphics Triennale, Fredrikstad, Norway, Grand Prix
1993	International Graphics Triennale, Giza, Egypt, Gold Medal
1994	Recommended for Augsburg, Grand Prix International Print Triennale, Krakow, Regulation Prize

Works in Collections

Muzeum Narodowe, Krakow
Muzeum Narodowe, Warsaw
Muzeum Sztuki, Lodz
Muzeum Okregowe, Radom
Muzeum Okregowe, Lublin
Muzeum Okregowe, Bydgoszcz
Museum of Contemporary Art, Lille, France
Art Centre, Kyoto, Japan
Kunsthalle, Nürnberg, Germany
Graphische Sammlung Albertina, Vienna, Austria
Mayor of Habikino, Osaka, Japan

Bibliography

The following publications have been of assistance during the research and writing of this book:

Artystychnych, B. W., *100 lat Polskiej Sztuki Plakatu* (*100 Years of Polish Poster Art*), Krzysztof Dydo, Krakow, 1993.

Davies, N., *God's Playground: On Visiting Alice's Polish Wonderland*, Universitas, Krakow, 1995.

1 Miedzynarodowe Triennale Grafiki — Kolor w Grafice (catalogue), Panstwowa Galeria Sztuki WOZOWNIA, Torun, 1994.

Jezioranski, J. N., *Poland after Communism*, Universitas, Krakow, 1995.

Luczynska, Z., *Jewish Kazimierz Short Guide* (trans. Krzysztof Zarzycki), Argona Jordan Art and Previa Editions, Krakow.

Milosz, C., *On Contrasts in Poland*, Universitas, Krakow, 1995.

Muthesius, S., *Art, Architecture and Design in Poland* (English edn), Verlag Langewiesche Nachfolger, Konigstein im Taunus, 1994.

'New Art from Eastern Europe — Identity and Conflict', *Art & Design Magazine*, (Special issue), London, 1994.

Oberhuber, K. & Pokay, P., *Polnische Graphik in der Albertina*, Graphische Sammlung Albertina, Vienna, 1993.

Salter, M. & McLachlan, G., *Poland — The Rough Guide*, Harper Columbus, London, 1991.

Triennale '91 and Intergrafia '91 (catalogues), Miedzynarodowe Triennale Grafiki, Krakow, 1991.

Triennale '94 and Intergrafia '94, (catalogues), Miedzynarodowe Triennale Grafiki, Krakow, 1994.

Wierzchowska, W., *Wspolczesny Rysunek Polski* (*Polish Contemporary Drawing*), Angiya Oficyna Wydawnicza, Warsaw, 1982.